# *Acknowledgements*

The creation of this book would not have been possible without the help of so many individuals. The author and publisher want to express their deepest gratitude in particular to the architects, designers, owners, and public relations personnel who, despite repeated requests for material and information from the author, never seized to be cooperative and supportive, and for allowing us to introduce the restaurants they designed/own to readers around the world. Many thanks also to the offices and photographers who gave us permission to use their photographs for this book. We furthermore want to emphasize our appreciation to Junichi Yanagisawa, for taking the time despite his busy schedule and a family waiting for him to do that great Japanese copywriting for every single restaurant of this book.

As the author of this book, I want to especially thank Adelien Vandeweghe who designed this beautiful layout and editor Elaine Lee for their great teamwork. It has been a pleasure to work with you. Furthermore, I want to say thank you to my Japanese friends and to my husband for their everlasting encouragement and support.

Author's remark:

There are different systems for spelling Japanese words in Roman characters. A name spelled Katsunori in this book might be spelled Katunori in other publications. Words like shochu, might be written shouchuu, or even sotyuu elsewhere. The Romanization used in this book is the most commonly used in modern publications. However, names of people or company names received from the designer's offices were not changed.

Japanese names stated in this book are written in the Western system of first names first and surnames last.

THE DRAGON KING INVITES YOU TONIGHT TO HIS WORLD FULL OF FANTASY, ADVENTURE, AND DELIGHT.

WITH ITS AMAZING CHARM, THIS ROOM TAMES THE DARKNESS' DREADFUL GLOOM.

WELCOME TO TEMARI'S WORLD WHERE GENTLENESS, COMFORT AND JOY IS UNFURLED.

ENJOY THE MOMENT, ENJOY THE NIGHT AND SURRENDER TO THE TWINKLING STARS' ENCHANTING LIGHT.

JAPANESE PATTERNS ENVELOPE THE GUEST WITH GENEROSITY AT ITS BEST.

FEEL THE GREAT SENSATION OF THIS ANCIENT HOME WHERE YAOYOROZU'S SPIRITS ROAM.

A FOOD STADIUM'S STAGE THAT SURELY IS IMPERIAL, CRAFTSMEN CO ACT WITH RAW MATERIAL.

WHERE CHARMING ATMOSPHERE OF SPACE OVERFLOWS YOU WITH GRACE.

COMPLETELY EMBRACED BY TENDER RAIN - A MOMENT OF STILLNESS.

BEING EMBRACED AND PROTECTED BY SOLID EARTH IS HEALING – ENJOY THIS WONDERFUL FEELING.

DELICIOUS FOOD AND FELICITY RESULTS FROM THIS STAGE'S ELEGANT SIMPLICITY.

A SPACE FULL OF MYSTERY, IN WHICH SYMBOLS, TRADITION, AND REALITY COEXIST IN HARMONY.

ALWAYS CHARMING IS ONE DUTY OF THIS BEWITCHING BEAUTY.

YOUR HEART LEAPS WHEN YOU BEFRIEND WITH THESE FANTASTIC SPIRITS WHO DESCEND ON THIS BEWITCHING PLACE.

IN THIS ORGANIC WORLD FULL OF AFFECTION LIVES OKINAWA'S SPIRIT OF PROTECTION.

WITH ITS MANY FACES OF WAVES AND COLLABORATING CIRCLES, THIS INTERIOR SURELY APPEARS SUPERIOR.

GETTING DRUNK INSIDE A WINE BARREL – IT'S TIME TO DREAM.

ADMIRE THE BEAUTY BEFORE THE DAWN OF LIGHT - THAT DANCES, FLOATS AND RISES WITH THE WIND TONIGHT.

LIKE A FAIRY TALE SO SUBLIME, ENJOY THIS PRECIOUS TIME - DEEP BELOW THE SEA.

GAZING AT THE FLOWERS BLOOMING ON THE MOON – TRANQUILITY WILL SOOTHE YOU SOON.

SO ELEGANT A PLACE CAN ONLY BE WITH JAPANESE STYLE, DELICACY AND A PINCH OF FANTASY.

CRAFTED WITH FIRE, WOOD, AND IRON – YET SO FLEXIBLE AND TENDER – THIS SPACE IS FULL OF SPLENDOUR.

A MAGNIFICENT MOMENT IS BORN INTO THIS PLACE FULL OF FLOWERS.

A GLITTERING BOX FILLED WITH EUROPEAN MAGNIFICENCE.

ONLY INSIDE SUCH A BEAUTIFUL CREATION CAN BE DISCOVERED THE UTTER RELAXATION.

IN THIS CAPTIVATING SPACE OF DELIGHT - CALL OUT FOR PRINCESS KAGUYA TONIGHT.

THE BLACK ROSE'S LIGHT ENHANCES THE BEAUTY OF THE NIGHT - ENJOY THIS MOMENT OF DELIGHT.

ENJOY THIS INTERIOR'S FINE QUALITY UNTIL YOU STEP BACK OUT INTO REALITY WHERE YOU CAN STILL FEEL THE ELEGANCE AND SORROW

THAT REMAINED FROM THE ANCIENT RED LIGHT DISTRICT OF GION AND WILL STILL LINGER THERE IN THE MORROW.

THE NIGHT RULES OVER THIS UNUSUALLY DIMENSIONED SPACE OF MEDIEVAL TIMES' FASCINATION AND GRACE.

ENWRAPPED IN THE TENDER FLAKES OF SNOW THAT IS FALLING – SAVOUR THE NIGHT THAT IS CALLING.

PUT BEHIND TIME AND SORROW - SPEND THE NIGHT IN ALICE'S WONDERLAND TILL THE WAKE OF THE MORROW.

DIVE INTO THE WATERFALL OF LIGHT, GET AWAY FROM IT ALL AND ENJOY THE MOMENT OF DELIGHT.

THE ORGANIC BEAUTY OF NATURAL WOOD MAKES RELAXATION FEEL SO GOOD.

FOLLOW THE NIGHT'S CALL AND SPEND TIME IN THIS CRIMSON RED ETERNAL FALL.

SAVOUR THE TENDERNESS, BEAUTY, AND PASSION IN THE ANCIENT RYUKYU KINGDOM'S FASHION.

SHINING NOT ONLY FROM THE CEILINGS THESE THOUSAND LAMPLIGHTS CREATE NOSTALGIC FEELINGS.

EVERYTHING PULSATES IN THIS WORLD – A SPIRITUAL MOVEMENT UNFURLED.

詩 *Poems* TRANSLATION

008	THAI THAI OKINAWA
014	AOBA-TEI
020	NANAIRO TEMARIUTA
024	DAZZLE
028	UTSUWA
032	SAIZO
036	BISHOKU MAIMON
040	SAN NEN BUTA-ZO
044	OTOOTO
050	THE STRANGER
056	SIMPATICA
060	LE PORC DE VERSAILLES
064	ALUX
068	THAI THAI YAMAGATA
074	BU'SA
080	MAIMON
084	SHIROKAKUYA
088	HIRARI
092	LUXIS
098	GETS'KA
104	IKKI
108	ROBUTAYA
114	TUBOMI
120	THE WIZARD OF THE OPERA
126	KADOSHIKA
132	TAKETORI 100 MONOGATARI
138	KAKUZAN
142	GION-RO
146	HARDEN TIGHTEN
150	KAMAKURA
154	ALICE'S LABYRINTH
158	TEIRYOU
162	YUI
166	KOYOSHIGURE
170	YANBARU
174	SEOUL SOUL
180	UGOKU MACHI

ZOUKEI SYUDAN CO, LTD, ITOU BUILDING 2F, 1-8-3 EBISU, SHIBUYA-KU, TOKYO 150-0013

ATELIER HITOSHI ABE, 3-3-16 OROSHIMACHI, WAKABAYASHI-KU, MIYAGI –KEN, SENDAI 984-0015

CALM.DESIGN CO, LTD, DAISAN-MARUYONE BUILDING 215, 4-6-17 BAKUROMACHI, CHUO-KU, OSAKA 541-0059

ATTA CO, LTD, #301, 2-28-7 EBISU, SHIBUYA-KU, TOKYO 150-0013

DESCARTES INC, 2-4-10, 2F, SHIBUYA, SHIBUYA-KU, TOKYO 150-0002

TAMO DESIGN AND ENGINEERING, 3-1-5-1F NISHI-GOTANDA, SHINAGAWA-KU, TOKYO 141-0031

CAFÉ CO, SIX BLDG 2-11-13, MINAMIHORIE NISHI-KU, OSAKA 550-0015

FANTASTIC DESIGN WORKS, 401 MAISON MINAMI-AOYAMA, 5-18-4, MINAMIAOYAMA, MINATO-KU, TOKYO 107-0062

NOMURA CO, LTD, QIZ AOYAMA 3F, 3-39-5 JINGUMAE, SHIBUYA-KU, TOKYO 150-0001

HIDEO HORIKAWA ARCHITECT & ASSOCIATES, 3-22-3, AMANUMA, SUGINAMI-KU, TOKYO 167-0032

LOVE THE LIFE, 3-12-10-803, MOTO-ASAKUSA, TAITO-KU, TOKYO

FANTASTIC DESIGN WORKS, 401 MAISON MINAMI-AOYAMA, 5-18-4, MINAMI-AOYAMA, MINATO-KU, TOKYO 107-0062

FANTASTIC DESIGN WORKS, 401 MAISON MINAMI-AOYAMA, 5-18-4, MINAMI-AOYAMA, MINATO-KU, TOKYO 107-0062

ZOUKEI SYUDAN CO, LTD, ITOU BUILDING 2F, 1-8-3 EBISU, SHIBUYA-KU, TOKYO 150-0013

ZOUKEI SYUDAN CO, LTD, ITOU BUILDING 2F, 1-8-3 EBISU, SHIBUYA-KU, TOKYO 150-0013

CAFÉ CO, SIX BLDG 2-11-13, MINAMIHORIE NISHI-KU, OSAKA 550-0015

ZOUKEI SYUDAN CO, LTD, ITOU BUILDING 2F, 1-8-3 EBISU, SHIBUYA-KU, TOKYO 150-0013

BAYLEAF INC, 3F 12-19 DAIKANYAMACHO, SHIBUYA-KU, TOKYO 150-002

SOI, YOKOSHIBA 6 BLD, 5F 1-15-10 EBISU-NISHI, SHIBUYA-KU, TOKYO 150-0021

ZOUKEI SYUDAN CO, LTD, ITOU BUILDING 2F, 1-8-3 EBISU, SHIBUYA-KU, TOKYO 150-0013

BAYLEAF INC, 3F 12-19 DAIKANYAMACHO, SHIBUYA-KU, 150-002 TOKYO & DESCARTES INC, 2-4-10, 2F, SHIBUYA, SHIBUYA-KU, TOKYO 150-0002

ZOUKEI SYUDAN CO, LTD, ITOU BUILDING 2F, 1-8-3 EBISU, SHIBUYA-KU, TOKYO 150-0013

CALM.DESIGN CO, LTD, DAISAN-MARUYONE BUILDING 215, 4-6-17 BAKUROMACHI, CHUO-KU, OSAKA 541-0059

FANTASTIC DESIGN WORKS, 401 MAISON MINAMI-AOYAMA, 5-18-4, MINAMI-AOYAMA, MINATO-KU, TOKYO 107-0062

ZOUKEI SYUDAN CO, LTD, ITOU BUILDING 2F, 1-8-3 EBISU, SHIBUYA-KU, TOKYO 150-0013

FANTASTIC DESIGN WORKS, 401 MAISON MINAMI-AOYAMA, 5-18-4, MINAMI-AOYAMA, MINATO-KU, TOKYO 107-0062

SUPERMANIAC INC, 3F 2-2-2 TEMMA, KITA-KU, OSAKA 530-0043

ZOUKEI SYUDAN CO, LTD, ITOU BUILDING 2F, 1-8-3 EBISU, SHIBUYA-KU, TOKYO 150-0013

EMBODY DESIGN ASSOCIATION, 2F, 1-1-11 LABEL BLDG, NISHITENMA, KITA-KU, OSAKA 530-0047

STUDIO 4-SEKKEI, 964-1, OIMACHIOI, IRUMA-GUN, SAITAMA 356-0053

FANTASTIC DESIGN WORKS, 401 MAISON MINAMI-AOYAMA, 5-18-4, MINAMI-AOYAMA, MINATO-KU, TOKYO 107-0062

HASHIMOTO YUKIO DESIGN STUDIO INC, 4-2-5, SENDAGAYA, SHIBUYA-KU, TOKYO 151-0051

BAYLEAF INC, 3F 12-19 DAIKANYAMACHO, SHIBUYA-KU, 150-002 TOKYO & DESCARTES INC, 2-4-10, 2F, SHIBUYA, SHIBUYA-KU, TOKYO 150-0002

CALM.DESIGN CO, LTD, DAISAN-MARUYONE BUILDING 215, 4-6-17 BAKUROMACHI, CHUO-KU, OSAKA 541-0059

BAYLEAF INC, 3F 12-19 DAIKANYAMACHO, SHIBUYA-KU, TOKYO 150-002

ZOUKEI SYUDAN CO, LTD, ITOU BUILDING 2F, 1-8-3 EBISU, SHIBUYA-KU, TOKYO 150-0013

ZOUKEI SYUDAN CO, LTD, ITOU BUILDING 2F, 1-8-3 EBISU, SHIBUYA-KU, TOKYO 150-0013

Architects & Designers INDEX

デザイナー

008	THAI THAI OKINAWA
014	AOBA-TEI
020	NANAIRO TEMARIUTA
024	DAZZLE
028	UTSUWA
032	SAIZO
036	BISHOKU MAIMON
040	SAN NEN BUTA-ZO
044	OTOOTO
050	THE STRANGER
056	SIMPATICA
060	LE PORC DE VERSAILLES
064	ALUX
068	THAI THAI YAMAGATA
074	BU'SA
080	MAIMON
084	SHIROKAKUYA
088	HIRARI
092	LUXIS
098	GETS'KA
104	IKKI
108	ROBUTAYA
114	TUBOMI
120	THE WIZARD OF THE OPERA
126	KADOSHIKA
132	TAKETORI 100 MONOGATARI
138	KAKUZAN
142	GION-RO
146	HARDEN TIGHTEN
150	KAMAKURA
154	ALICE'S LABYRINTH
158	TEIRYOU
162	YUI
166	KOYOSHIGURE
170	YANBARU
174	SEOUL SOUL
180	UGOKU MACHI

900-0032沖縄県那覇市松山2-1-15沖縄サントリービル2階
980-0803宮城県仙台市青葉区国分町2-13-21
160-0022東京都新宿区新宿3-28-10ヒューマックスパビリオン新宿東口5F
104-0061東京都中央区銀座2-4-12ミキモトギンザ2 8F／9F
130-0022東京都墨田区江東橋4-28-2 1F
171-0021東京都豊島区西池袋1-13-1タグリート池袋B1F
530-0001大阪市北区梅田2-2-22ハービスENT5F
171-0022東京都豊島区南池袋2-16-8藤久ビル東3号館B1
150-6090東京都渋谷区恵比寿4-20-4恵比寿ガーデンプレイスグラススクエア
160-0021東京都新宿区歌舞伎町1-14-7ハヤシビル4F
225-0002神奈川県横浜市青葉区美しが丘2-17-12
103-0022東京都墨田区江東橋3-13-6KINSIAビル5F
107-0062港区南青山5-11-9レキシントン青山 B1F
990-0035山形県山形市小荷駄1-69
990-0039山形県山形市香澄町2-2-1大久保ビル1階
104-0061東京都中央区銀座8-3西土橋ビル1〜2F
373-0851群馬県太田市飯田町1190マルエスメガネ1階
150-0021東京都渋谷区恵比寿西1-16-8DROP IN代官山B1F
150-0021東京都渋谷区恵比寿西1-7-3ザインエビスビルB1F
041-0802北海道函館市石川町52番16号
330-0845埼玉県さいたま市大宮区仲町1-60アイス大宮ビルB1・B2
171-0022東京都豊島区南池袋1-20-3藤久ビル東2号館 地下1階
160-0022東京都新宿区新宿3-18-4セノビル5F
171-0022東京都豊島区南池袋2-16-8藤久ビル東3号館B1F
212-0027神奈川県川崎市幸区新塚越201
104-0061東京都中央区銀座6-5-15銀座能楽堂ビル6F鹿島田サウザンドモール2階
711-0911岡山県倉敷市小島小川町3671-7
605-0078京都府京都市東山区縄手富永町東入ル一筋目東北角タケトミビル 2F
106-0045東京都港区麻布十番1-9-2ユニマット麻布十番5F
105-0004東京都港区新橋3-23-1ボクサール新橋ビル 6F
104-0061東京都中央区銀座8-8-5太陽ビル5F
171-0021東京都豊島区西池袋1－40－5、名取ビルB1F
160-0022東京都新宿区新宿3-27-5ケースリービル3F
104-0061東京都中央区銀座6-13-3フロンティア銀座ビル2F
150-0002東京都渋谷区渋谷2-21-2第二田中ビルB1
990-0042山形県山形市七日町2丁目7-23オハラビル1階
901-2300沖縄県中城村字南上原945-1

Restaurants
ADDRESSES

レストラン

008	THAI THAI OKINAWA
014	AOBA-TEI
020	NANAIRO TEMARIUTA
024	DAZZLE
028	UTSUWA
032	SAIZO
036	BISHOKU MAIMON
040	SAN NEN BUTA-ZO
044	OTOOTO
050	THE STRANGER
056	SIMPATICA
060	LE PORC DE VERSAILLES
064	ALUX
068	THAI THAI YAMAGATA
074	BU'SA
080	MAIMON
084	SHIROKAKUYA
088	HIRARI
092	LUXIS
098	GETS'KA
104	IKKI
108	ROBUTAYA
114	TUBOMI
120	THE WIZARD OF THE OPERA
126	KADOSHIKA
132	TAKETORI 100 MONOGATARI
138	KAKUZAN
142	GION-RO
146	HARDEN TIGHTEN
150	KAMAKURA
154	ALICE'S LABYRINTH
158	TEIRYOU
162	YUI
166	KOYOSHIGURE
170	YANBARU
174	SEOUL SOUL
180	UGOKU MACHI

発想が動く、すべてに鼓動を感じる世界。

PHOTOGRAPHY	Masahiro Ishibashi
DESIGNER	Zoukei Syudan Co Ltd
DESIGN TEAM	Yusaku Kaneshiro, Hiromi Sato
CONTRACTOR	Mitano Create
ADDRESS	945-1 Minami-Uehara, Aza, Nakagusuku Village, Okinawa 901-2300
PHONE	+81 (0) 9 8895 2554
AREA	126 m²
SEATING	82 seats
COMPLETED	2005

183

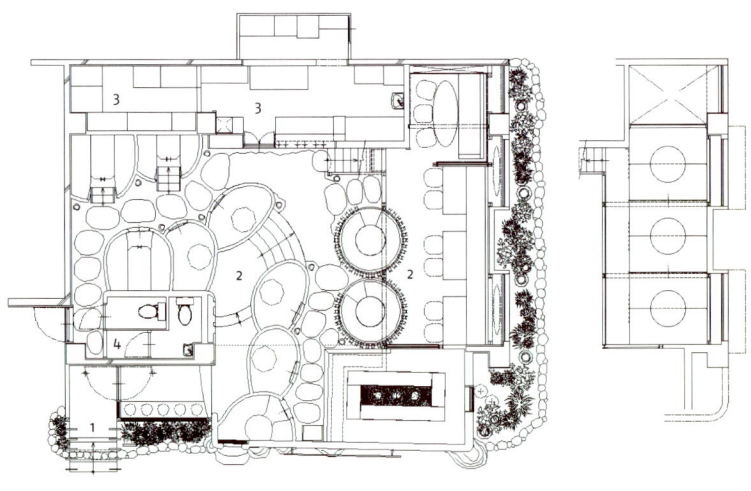

FLOORPLAN

1 entrance
2 dining area
3 kitchen
4 washroom

OKINAWA

沖縄　動く町

Ugoku Machi

Dining beyond the outer limits

It is no overstatement to say that Ugoku Machi is one of the strangest and most dazzling restaurants in the world. It certainly differs significantly from what people usually have in mind when they think of a restaurant. Ugoku Machi, which literally means "moving town", is located in Okinawa - Japan's beautiful archipelago located far south of the main island of Honshu, and native hometown of designer Yusaku Kaneshiro.

The restaurant's entrance area is staggered on the ground floor of a grey apartment building. An imposing wall imprinted with the word "Rocket", the huge surrounding stones and a rock with giant mushrooms certainly pique one's curiosity as to what the interior might be like.

Stepping through the wooden door, guests are transported into an unfamiliar world. Sand, fragments of brick, wooden boards and large stones alternate to form footbridges for guests to stroll through this strange territory. As with most of the restaurants designed by Kaneshiro, comfortable private booths are scattered along the way for guests to enjoy privacy as they dine. These eclectic booths resemble stone igloos and little metallic space ships, plated with junkyard finds such as computer chips, exhaust pipes and other unidentifiable scraps. One of these pieces even resembles a serpent's carcass when laid out as a centrepiece on the table, proving that even scraps can function well as works of art.

PHOTOGRAPHY	Masahiro Ishibashi
DESIGNER	Zoukei Syudan Co., Ltd.
DESIGN TEAM	Yusaku Kaneshiro, Mitsuru Komatsuzaki
CONTRACTOR	Gendai-Kikaku
ADDRESS	Ohara Bldg. 1F, 2-7-23 Nanoka-machi, Yamagata City, Yamagata 990-0042
PHONE	+81 (0) 2 3629 8766
AREA	269 m²
SEATING	137 seats
COMPLETED	2005

177

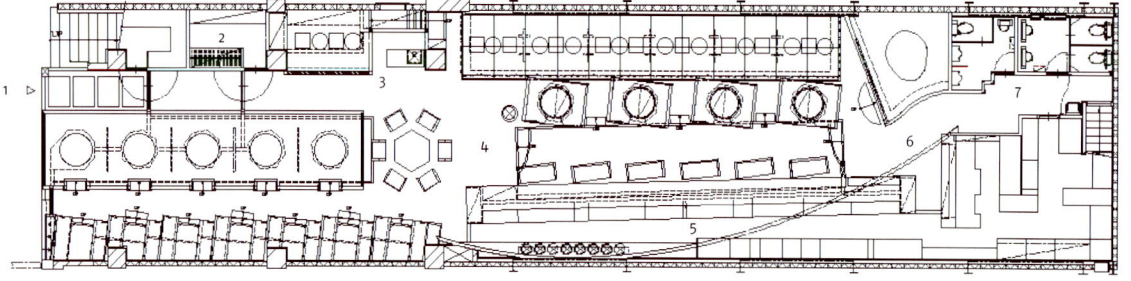

FLOORPLAN

1 entrance
2 staff room
3 cashier
4 dining area
5 kitchen
6 bar
7 washroom

その幾千の灯火は、集う人の郷愁を誘う。

山形

ソウルソウル

Seoul Soul

Feasting between Korean Hangul characters & cubes

While the name of the restaurant and the variety of "Hangul" characters on its exterior walls inform the curious that Seoul Soul serves Korean food, the interior reveals so much more. The fusion of traditional and modern influences shows in the way the characters are illuminated and decorated. This extends to the design of the whole interior, especially the cubicle booths. While the modern influence is evident, it does not overwhelm the Korean ambience. Designer Yusaku Kaneshiro was assigned to make the most of a small budget for this restaurant and he clearly did a great job.

The main highlights of the interior are its cubicle booths, with one for each customer. Within each booth, illuminated, colourful glass cubes supporting a glass tabletop attract the eye instantly when one walks into the dining area. Other surrounding cubic sculptures are also illuminated from within and incorporate "Hangul" characters. At the bar, these cubicle booths offer couples an alternative place for interaction, instead of the usual uncomfortable barstool. Inside, they can chat and drink in a romantic and private atmosphere, uninterrupted by anyone - except the bartenders.

Elsewhere in the restaurant, the Tatami area offers a more traditional setting, where guests can sit on traditional Korean stools instead of sitting on the floor, as they usually do in Japan. However, the Hangul on one of the walls and the numerous ceiling lamps reflected and amplified in mirrors on the other walls add a special contrasting impact. The lamps are actually typical, inexpensive lamps that have been dismounted and attached to the ceiling.

古代琉球の優しさと激しさと美しさを味わう。

PHOTOGRAPHY	Hiroshi Tsujitani (Nacasa & Partners Inc.)
DESIGNER	Bayleaf Inc.
DESIGN TEAM	Taro Maeda
CONTRACTOR	Tecno
ADDRESS	B1 #2 Tanaka Bldg, 2-21-2 Shibuya, Shibuya-ku, Tokyo 150-0002
PHONE	+81 (0) 3 5468 5898
AREA	81 m²
SEATING	48 seats
COMPLETED	2004

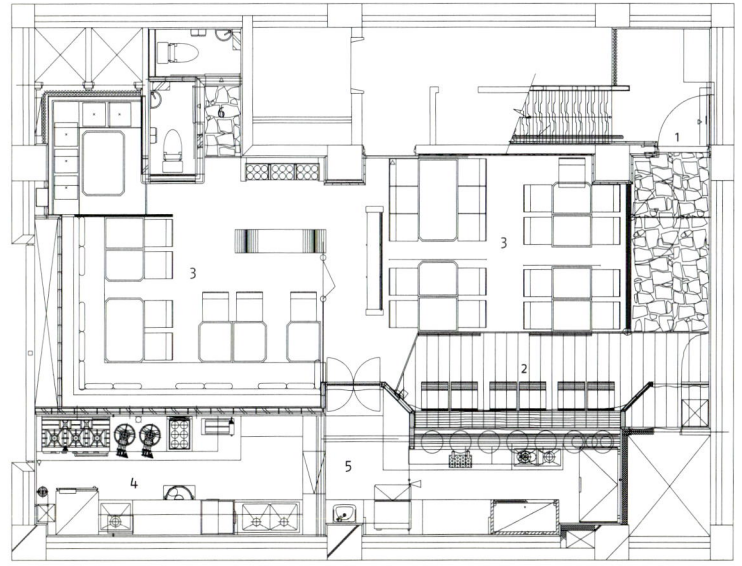

SECOND FLOOR

1. entrance
2. counter
3. dining area
4. kitchen
5. pantry
6. washroom

東京

やんばる

Yanbaru

Savouring sake by the forest stream

The name Yanbaru is derived from Yanbarukuina, a bird that is native to Okinawa. It lives in the forest and is used as a motif for this restaurant. Designer Taro Maeda modelled the interior after the image of a sakagura, a traditional Japanese sake brewery where sake is stored.

A stream of water flows between the benches and the wall in one part of the restaurant. Through illumination from below and the movement of the water, a beautifully flickering image is projected onto the wall and ceiling. The idea was to replicate the image of clean water flowing through a forest, since fresh and clean water is obviously crucial for brewing delicious sake, and sake breweries were often built directly next to a stream. The pattern on the wall depicts a forest in which some Yanbarukuina can be found.

At the counter, guests will discover an interesting feature – the photos of old Okinawa designed to look like an enlarged film strip. Maeda used authentic old photographs of Okinawan buildings as well as past scenes from the lives of Okinawan people. These photos can be borrowed from a public facility in Okinawa that collects such old photographs.

Circular Ryukyu glass lamps made in Okinawa hang from the ceiling and beautifully enhance the atmosphere of the room. Two steel lamps mounted on the wall are just as appealing – each embossed with the outline of the Okinawa Rail network that becomes visible through the illumination. Yanbaru's menu consists mainly of Okinawan food and Awamori, the famous Okinawan shochu.

FIRST FLOOR

1 entrance
2 dining area
3 kitchen
4 washroom

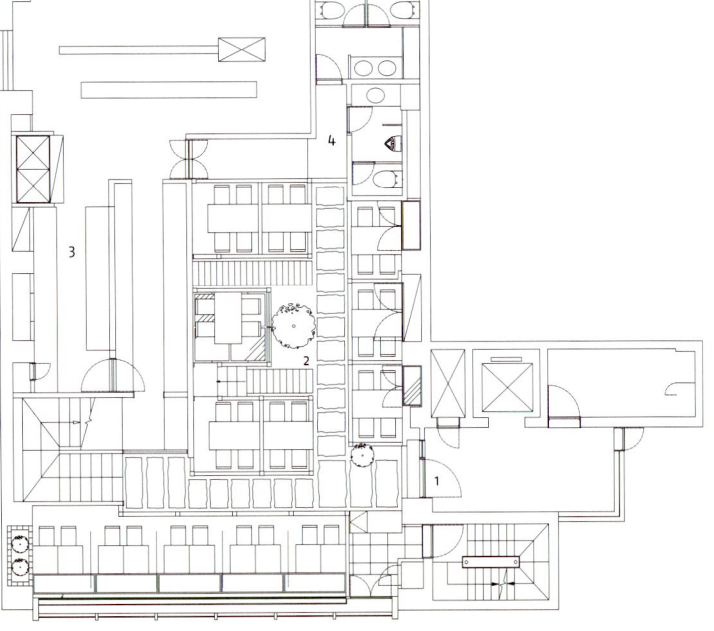

PHOTOGRAPHY	Hirokazu Matsuoka
DESIGNER	calm.design co., ltd.
DESIGN TEAM	Takuya Kanazawa
CONTRACTOR	Diamond Dining
ADDRESS	Frontier Ginza Building 2F/3F, 6-13-3 Ginza, Chuo-ku, Tokyo 104 0061
PHONE	+81 (0) 3 5565 7100
AREA	300 m²
SEATING	180 seats, 16 private rooms
COMPLETED	2005

その永遠の秋は愉しみの時を、紅に染める。

東京

紅葉時雨

Koyoshigure
Where autumn visits everyday

Koyoshigure is a combination of "kouyou", meaning autumn colours and "shigure", a special word for late autumn Japanese rain showers. Together, it means "a shower of red autumn leaves".

Upon entering the restaurant, the rationale behind the name becomes clear. Guests would feel as if they had travelled back in time and space to a small ancient village during late autumn – even during hot summer. Private dining areas resemble small houses, laid out across a network of small "streets" made up of square stepping-stones surrounded by pebbles.

Leaves dyed in scarlet and vermilion flutter and scatter about the floor, but the real centrepiece is a three-metre, autumn-coloured maple tree that beautifully enhances the whole atmosphere. Small lamps on the floor and in front of the "houses" emit soft light that blend perfectly with the rest of the interior.

The little houses have round or squared windows and red curtains at the entrance so that guests can dine in seclusion. The other private rooms are on a higher level that can be reached by a small flight of stairs. They are built on stilts, like the houses of ancient times, and from any one of them, diners can gaze directly at the tree. Bigger private rooms are located on the other floor of the establishment. One Tatami room accommodates up to 40 guests and is mainly used for company festivities. Every room is individually designed with scenes of fire, snow, water, wind, and light in combination with the autumnal theme.

FLOORPLAN
1 entrance
2 dining area
3 counter
4 kitchen
5 washroom

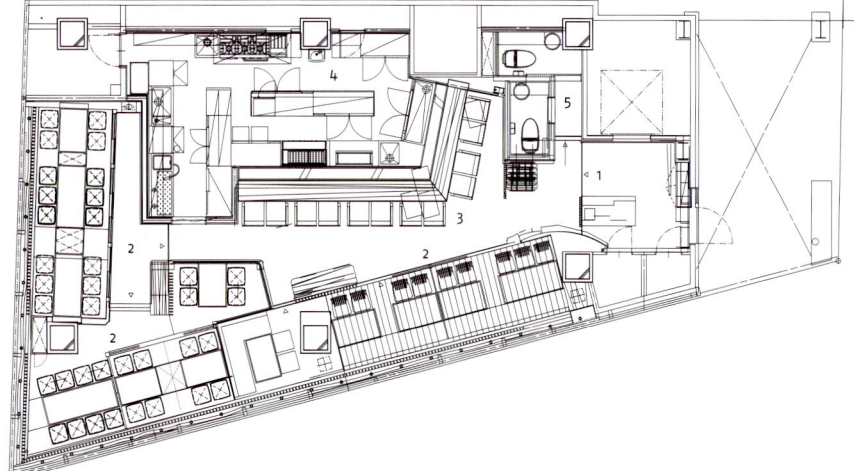

PHOTOGRAPHY	Hiroshi Tsujitani (Nacasa & Partners Inc.)
DESIGNER	Bayleaf Inc. & Descartes Inc.
DESIGN TEAM	Taro Maeda, Noriko Amemiya, Katsuhiko Yamamoto
CONTRACTOR	Sun Royal co. ltd.
ADDRESS	K3 Building 3F, 3-27-5 Shinjuku, Shinjuku-ku, Tokyo 160-0022
PHONE	+81 (0) 3 3355 3131
AREA	115 m²
SEATING	71 seats, 3 private rooms
COMPLETED	2005

天然木の素直で美しい直線が生むやすらぎ。

東京

結 *Yui*

Dining under the copper moon

This robata restaurant is located in a district around Shinjuku station that offers many department stores as well as a bustling nightlife filled mostly with younger Tokyoites who appreciate the myriad choices of restaurants and bars.

Yui's entrance at the cash register counter is already a visual experience, with beautiful illumination from below, and lined with a handpicked Obi decorated with different patterns. This leads on to a path paved with traditional straw rice bags ("komedawara") that complement the dark stone tiles very well.

Another visual feature that stands out is the copper red half moon-shaped motifs that serve to separate the different spaces. These are made from stainless steel that is scratched, varnished (applied with an airbrush) and then burned. Ryukyu glass lamps light up the scenery exquisitely, enhancing the copper colour even more.

At the counter, double seats invite couples to sit down and watch the chefs prepare the food. From behind it looks as if two chairs were just casually put together; however, they were created so that there would be no awkward armrest in the middle. Diners can choose from a decorative selection of fish speared on sticks above the counter.

In one of the private seating areas, tabletops are covered with a graphic sheet of red flowers and bamboo that look like pieces of art. In addition, the Japanese Shoji structures attached to the windows offer just as much sophistication; these are illuminated from within but not all at the same time - a timer switches the light from one pane to another.

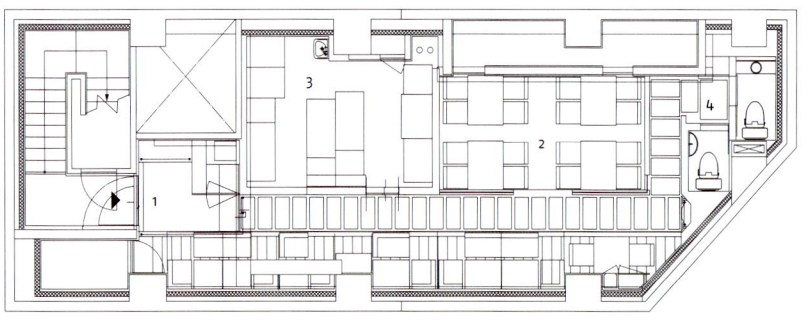

FLOORPLAN

1 entrance
2 dining area
3 kitchen
4 washroom

PHOTOGRAPHY	Jun Nakamichi (Nacasa & Partners Inc.)
DESIGNER	Hashimoto Yukio Design Studio Inc.
DESIGN TEAM	Yukio Hashimoto, Mariko Iwata
CONTRACTOR	O.D.S. Inc.
ADDRESS	B1F, Natori Bldg., 1-40-5, Nishi Ikebukuro, Toshima-ku, Tokyo 171-0021
PHONE	+81 (0) 3 5949 5778
AREA	62 m²
SEATING	30 seats
COMPLETED	2004

光の瀧を潜り、日常を忘れ、やすらぎの時へ。

東京

庭燎

Teiryou

Parting the curtain of light

The owner requested designer Yukio Hashimoto to conceptualise the interior for a restaurant focused on secluded dining areas. Hashimoto knew that if he integrated walls to create partitions, the space would feel too cramped. Therefore he wanted to use soft and flexible material – a material that would give the space individuality as well.

Traditional Japanese restaurants usually mark their entrances with a noren, a curtain or room divider with vertical slits to make it easier to walk through. The designer came up with the idea to create a futuristic noren and experimented with optical fibres. These were inserted into vinyl chloride tubes and then hung from the ceiling along the hallway in the restaurant. Since the tubes are pliable, guests can walk through to the tables, but from the hallway it becomes a shining sheer wall without any unsightly gaps. The beautiful effect of the light curtain is enhanced through a harmonic combination with the stone paved floor and the Oya stone walls. Oya stones are popular and have been used for hundreds of years in Japanese interiors because they absorb odours and moisture. This perfect balance helped Hashimoto to create a beautifully calm and composed space where guests can enjoy modern Japanese dishes while enjoying the ambience of this very special restaurant.

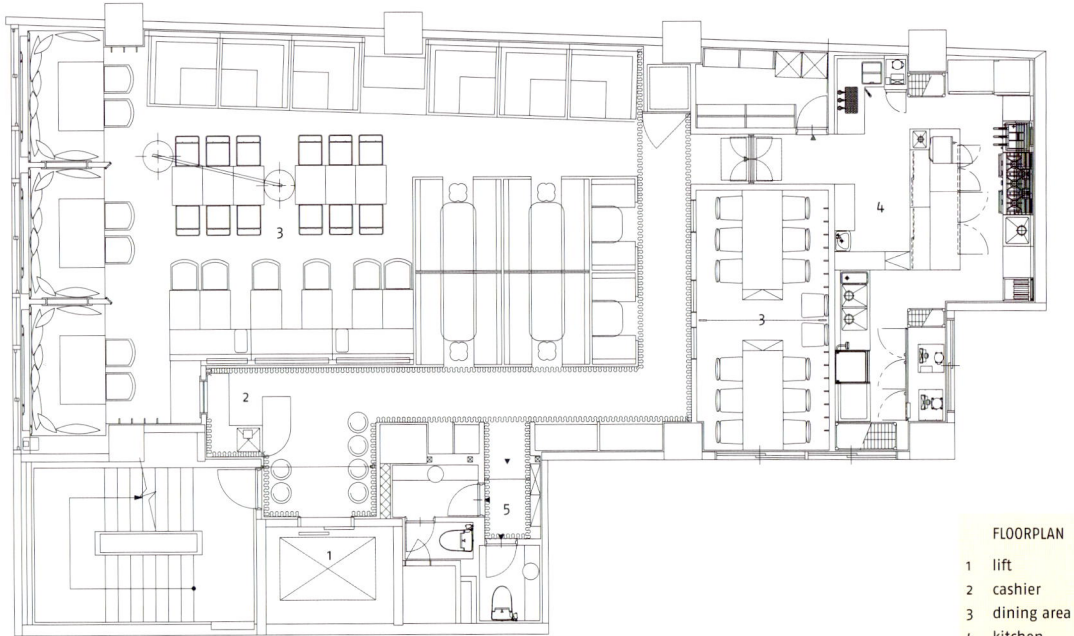

FLOORPLAN

1 lift
2 cashier
3 dining area
4 kitchen
5 washroom

PHOTOGRAPHY	Nacasa & Partners Inc.
DESIGNER	Fantastic Design Works
DESIGN TEAM	Katsunori Suzuki
CONTRACTOR	Diamond Dining
ADDRESS	Taiyo Bldg. 5F, 8-8-5 Ginza, Chuo-ku, Tokyo 104-0061
PHONE	+81 (0) 3 3574 6980
AREA	182 m²
SEATING	110 seats
COMPLETED	2003

今宵不思議の国へ誘われ、時を忘れ我を忘れる。

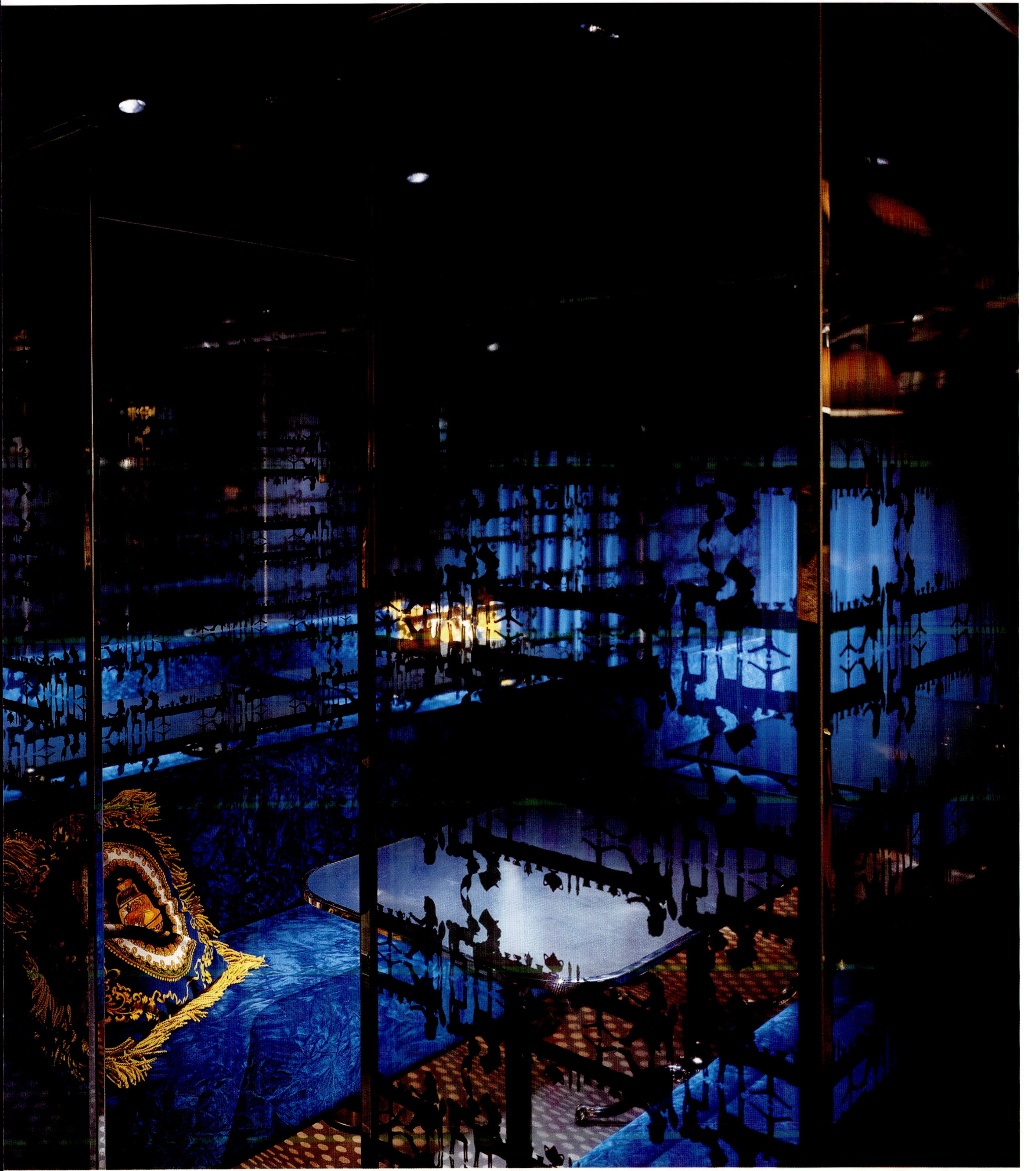

東京

迷宮の国のアリス

Alice's Labyrinth
Of fantasy forests and mad tea parties

With fairy tale and manga-loving designer Katsunori Suzuki, it's no surprise that the theme of this restaurant is based on Lewis Carroll's fantasy book "Alice's Adventures in Wonderland". Fantasy extends beyond the interior design, right down to the waitress uniform, a mix of girly Lolita style and French maid uniform. Here, waitresses must look and act cute. In recent years maid cafés and cosplay (from "costume play") restaurants have gained in popularity, where waitresses or waiters dress up in costumes. The concept started in Akihabara, a district of Tokyo that is well known not only for the masses of shops selling electric goods, but also for being the capital of manga fans. Now such establishments can be found all over Tokyo and in other cities as well.

Alice's Labyrinth has different private rooms designed and named after the various scenes from Alice's Wonderland. There is the "fantasy forest," a forest where everything grows headfirst – or at least the tree graphics on the wall and the ceiling lamps that resemble differently coloured flower buds. The 'tea party" is another interesting room, obviously borrowing from the Mad Hatter's famous "tea party". The low-key lighting, the creative structures and the patterns on the carpets, the walls, or glass dividers definitely help guests to imagine themselves in an alternative fantasy world.

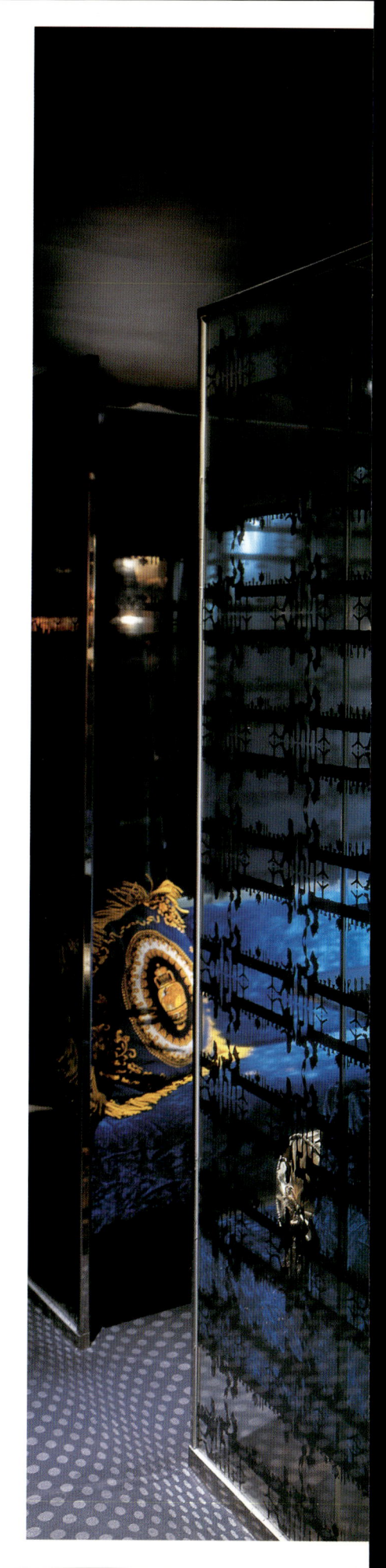

FLOORPLAN
1. lift
2. entrance
3. dining area
4. kitchen
5. pantry
6. counter
7. washroom

PHOTOGRAPHY	Ellen Nepilly
DESIGNER	Isao Hosoya
DESIGN TEAM	Studio 4-Sekkei
CONTRACTOR	Rincrew
ADDRESS	3-23-1 Bokusaru Shinbashi Bldg. 6F, Shinbashi, Minato-ku, Tokyo 105-0004
PHONE	+81 (0) 3 5777 2977
AREA	324 m²
SEATING	170 seats
COMPLETED	2004

降り積もる雪の優しさに包まれ、味わう夜。

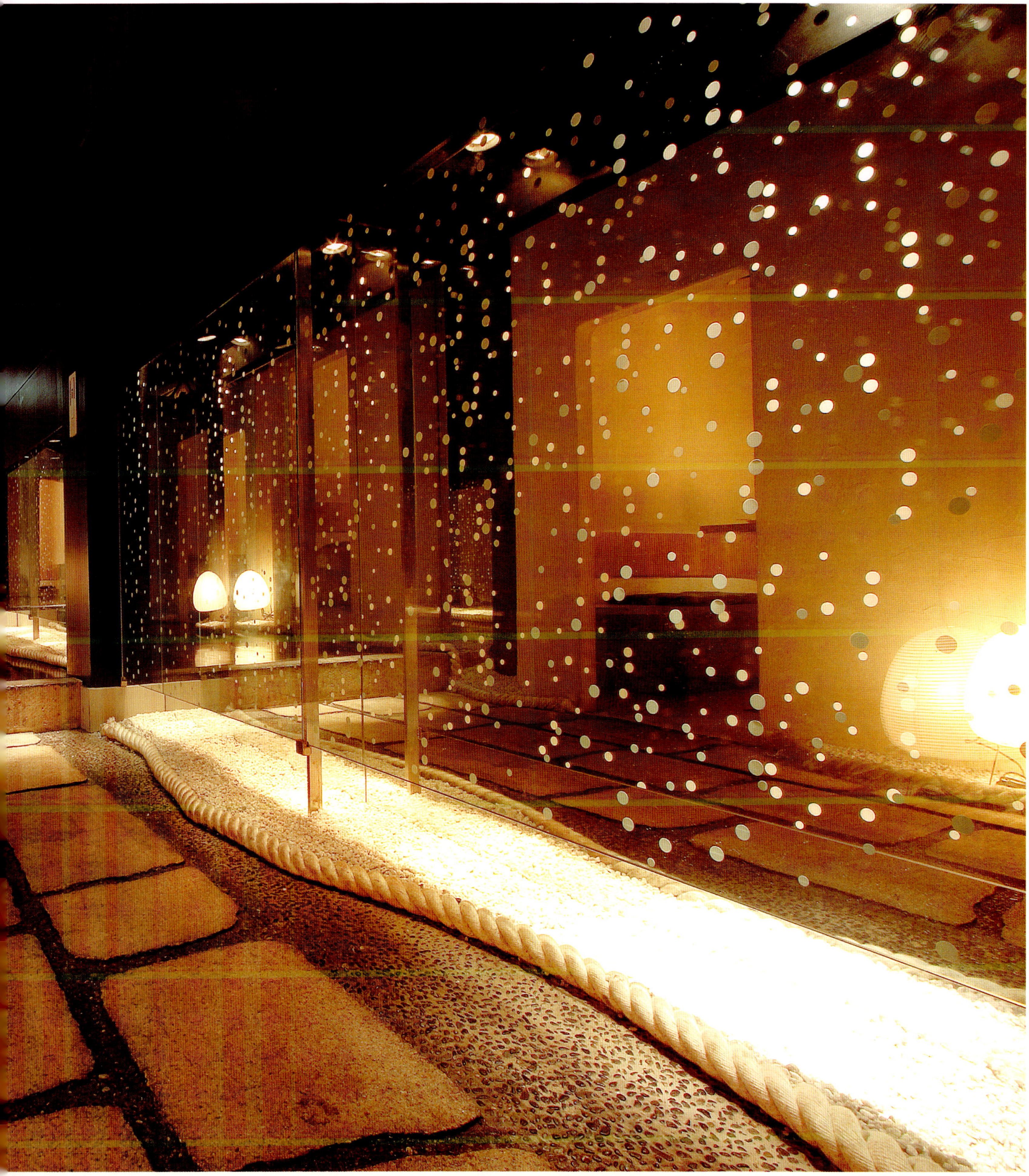

東京

かまくら

Kamakura

Enjoying winter's first snowfall in mini-land

After stooping through Kamakura's tiny entrance door, incoming guests may wonder if they have accidentally entered the set for Snow White and the Seven Dwarfs. Dining booths look like the houses of a mini town. The little huts are actually cubicles with one table in the middle and a bench around it. Small groups of up to eight persons can sit comfortably opposite one another and converse with everyone at the table, creating a unique and memorable dining experience.

The white dots painted on a glass panel along the hallway next to the huts create the impression of winter's first snowfall. This image, combined with the warm illumination of the rice paper lamps, is quite captivating and results in an even cosier feeling within the cubicles.

The other section of the restaurant includes regular private rooms and Japanese styled rooms, which are designed to accommodate larger groups for company parties or similar functions. To be admitted to this section, guests must first take off their shoes and put them into specially provided racks that can be locked. There is also a counter window around the kitchen where diners can observe the chef broiling yakitori right before them.

PHOTOGRAPHY	Seiryo Yamada
DESIGNER	Embody Design Association
DESIGN TEAM	Katsuya Iwamoto
CONTRACTOR	D·factor
ADDRESS	Unimat Azabujuban 5F, 1-9-2, Azabujuban, Minato-ku, Tokyo 106-0045
PHONE	+81 (0) 3 6230 3313
AREA	39 m²
SEATING	60 seats
COMPLETED	2006

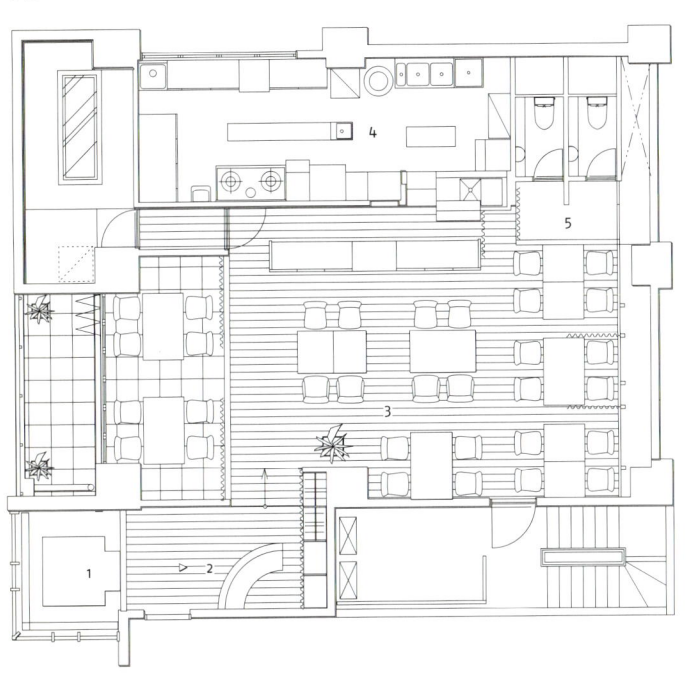

FIRST FLOOR
1 entrance
2 reception
3 dining area
4 kitchen
5 washroom

中世の典雅と妖艶が夜を支配する異次元空間。

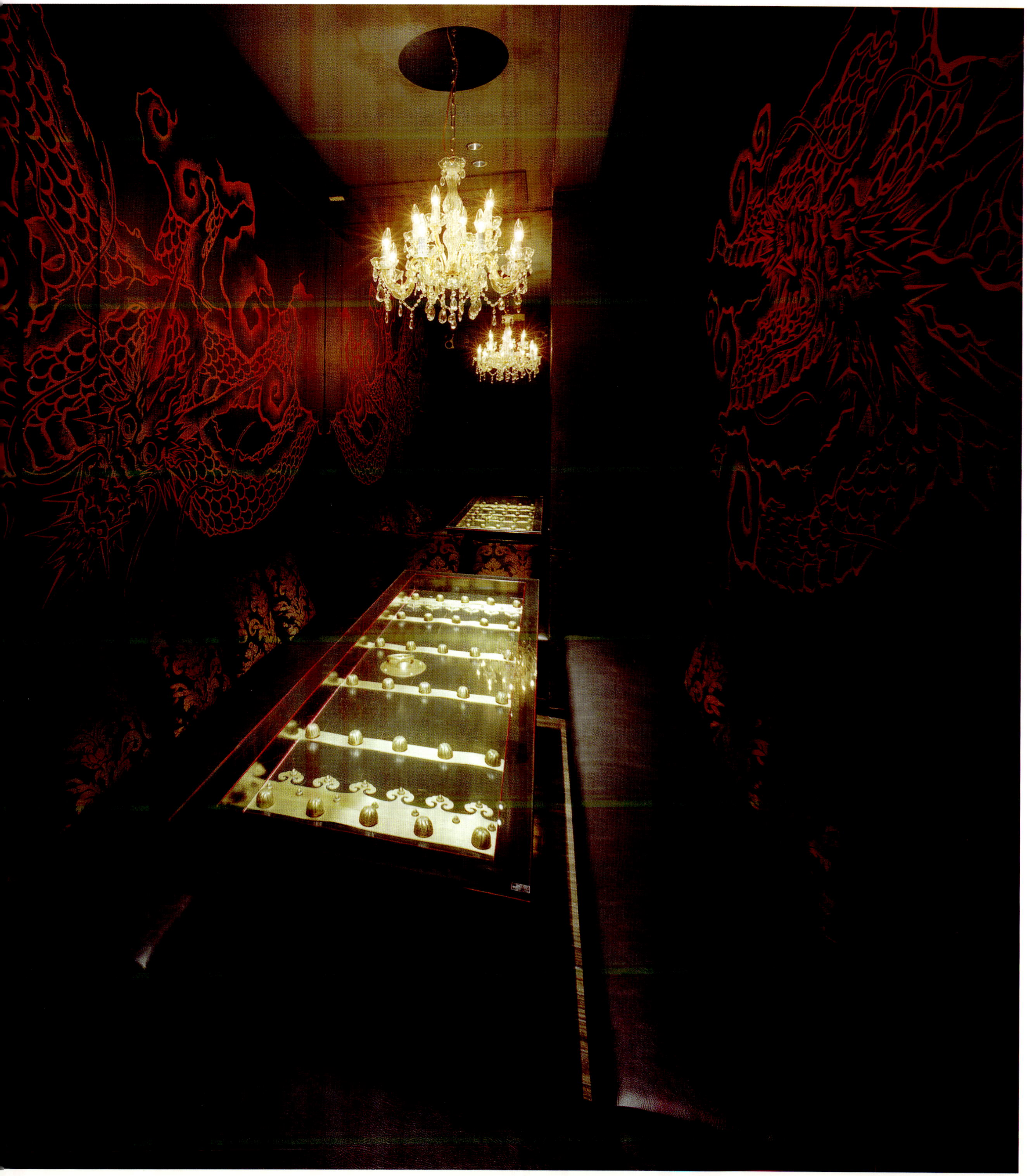

Harden Tighten

Dining with a little Shanghai spark

Harden Tighten is located in Azabujuban, a popular and traditional shopping town with many shops and restaurants that have stood for decades. Azabujuban was connected to the subway network only a few years ago; and with easier access, more people came to visit the area. Since then many new restaurants have opened; Harden Tighten is one of them. The goal of its interior design was to achieve an aesthetic beauty that would draw in locals and visitors alike.

With a Chinese kitchen, the interior motif would be inspired by contemporary Shanghai, leaning more towards the modern than the conservative. There is one main dining area and two private rooms with karaoke sets. Two red dragon graphics adorn the wall of the most outstanding private room, which hosts an impressive dining table made from a pane of glass mounted over an old Chinese door.

Other decorative highlights include wood panels with Chinese lattice patterns, which serve as partitions throughout the restaurant, while the wall mirrors sport intricate red graphics and the entrance area is lined with brown and black tiles in mosaic patterns. The vibrant red colour of the curtains and graphics help brighten up a dim space, while offering a sharp contrast to the dark wooden colours.

古の花街の優雅と哀愁、そして上質のある場所。

PHOTOGRAPHY	Takahiro Matsuo
DESIGNER	Zoukei Syudan Co., Ltd.
DESIGN TEAM	Yusaku Kaneshiro, Hiromi Sato
CONTRACTOR	Prosper
ADDRESS	Taketomi Bldg. 2F, Higashi-Hairu-Hitosujime, Higashikitakado, Nawate-Tominaga-cho, Higashiyama-ku, Kyoto 605-0078
PHONE	+81 (0) 7 5541 5300
AREA	125 m²
SEATING	56 seats
COMPLETED	2004

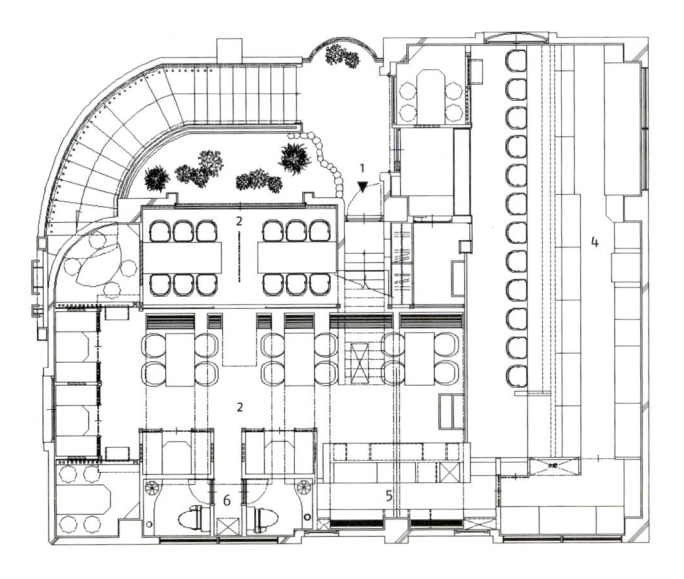

FLOORPLAN

1. entrance
2. dining area
3. kitchen
4. bar
5. washroom

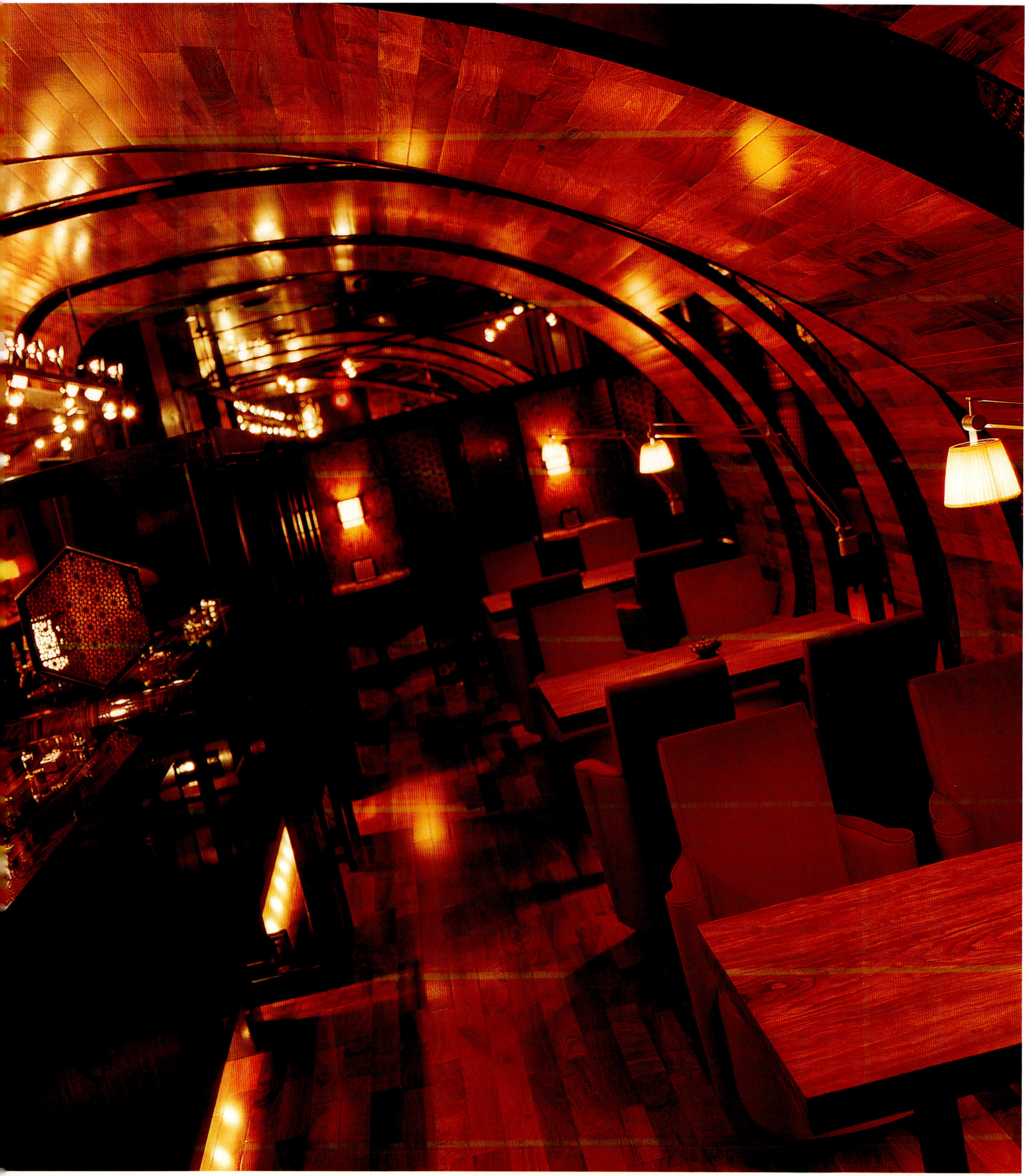

京都

祇園樓

Gion-ro

Relaxing in the warmth of old wood

Gion-ro is located in Kyoto's famous Gion and is one of designer Yusaku Kaneshiro's understated but appealing works. The interior's composition is just right for this area. Gion is a traditional pleasure district in which much of Japanese traditional architecture has survived the ravages of time. Many foreign tourists as well as Japanese from all over Japan come to visit the area. Walking through the streets and looking at the beautiful old houses certainly takes you back in time.

Kaneshiro skilfully designed the interior for this Chinese restaurant to aesthetically blend with its traditional Japanese surroundings. Moving up the staircase, one finds the restaurant very welcoming with its lampion-type lights. By using reddish coloured wood and indirect illumination, the atmosphere of the interior feels warm and comfortable. The bar counter area is enclosed with a wooden construction like a huge tunnel, thus creating an attractive and inviting partition. A long counter with red cosy-looking armchairs is especially attractive to guests who come alone. Furthermore, sitting at a counter does not make one feel as lonely as a huge table would. For couples, the option to dine next to each other works just as well. There are also four secluded areas with tables that seem specially designed for couples on a date.

PHOTOGRAPHY	Yoshihisa Araki
DESIGNER	Supermaniac Inc.
DESIGN TEAM	Nobuaki Suzuki
CONTRACTOR	Nobunori Miyamoto
ADDRESS	3671-7 Kojima Ogawa-cho, Kurashiki-city, Okayama 711-0911
PHONE	+81 (0) 8 6472 7322
AREA	206 m²
SEATING	101 seats
COMPLETED	2006

黒薔薇色の灯に映され、艶のある時を楽しむ。

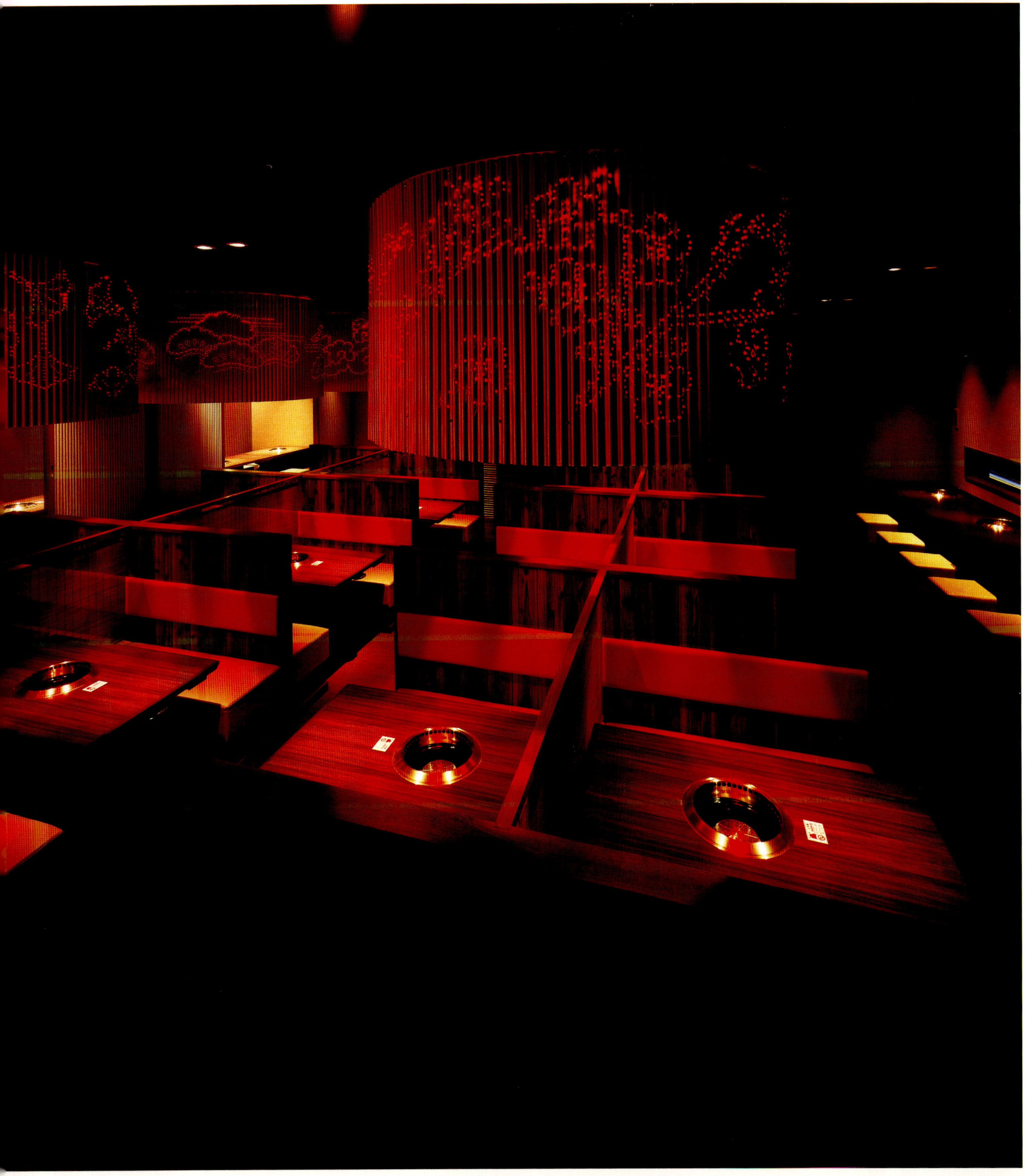

倉敷

鶴山

Kakuzan
Swinging in the '60s

Kakuzan's owner Nobunori Miyamoto still has his mother's image during the '60s in his mind - frantically working in the family's yakiniku restaurant that she had built from scratch. Yakiniku is a method of grilling meat, similar to barbeque. Like many houses and especially restaurants during that period in Japan, its walls were built with corrugated zinc panels. For Miyamoto, the '60s were a powerful period, which was also reflected in his mother's strength of character. He asked designer Nobuaki Suzuki to create a restaurant that not only reminded him of the old times but also offered something new. When designer Nobuaki Suzuki heard the owner's idea of the '60s and how the old restaurant was built, he decided to integrate corrugated zinc panels into the design.

Suzuki and his team used two layers of corrugated zinc panels and perforated them with holes on the outer layer depicting traditional Japanese motifs such as cranes, cherry blossoms, or ginkgo leaves. The inside of both layers was then coated red and illuminated from within, creating a calm interior that complements its stunning retro-modern space.

PHOTOGRAPHY	Masaya Yoshimura (Nacasa & Partners Inc.)
DESIGNER	Fantastic Design Works
DESIGN TEAM	Katsunori Suzuki
CONTRACTOR	Diamond Dining
ADDRESS	Ginza Nogakudo Bldg. 6F, 6-5-15 Ginza, Chuo-ku, Tokyo 104-0061
PHONE	+81 (0) 3 3574 5252
AREA	275 m²
SEATING	157 seats, 16 private rooms
COMPLETED	2004

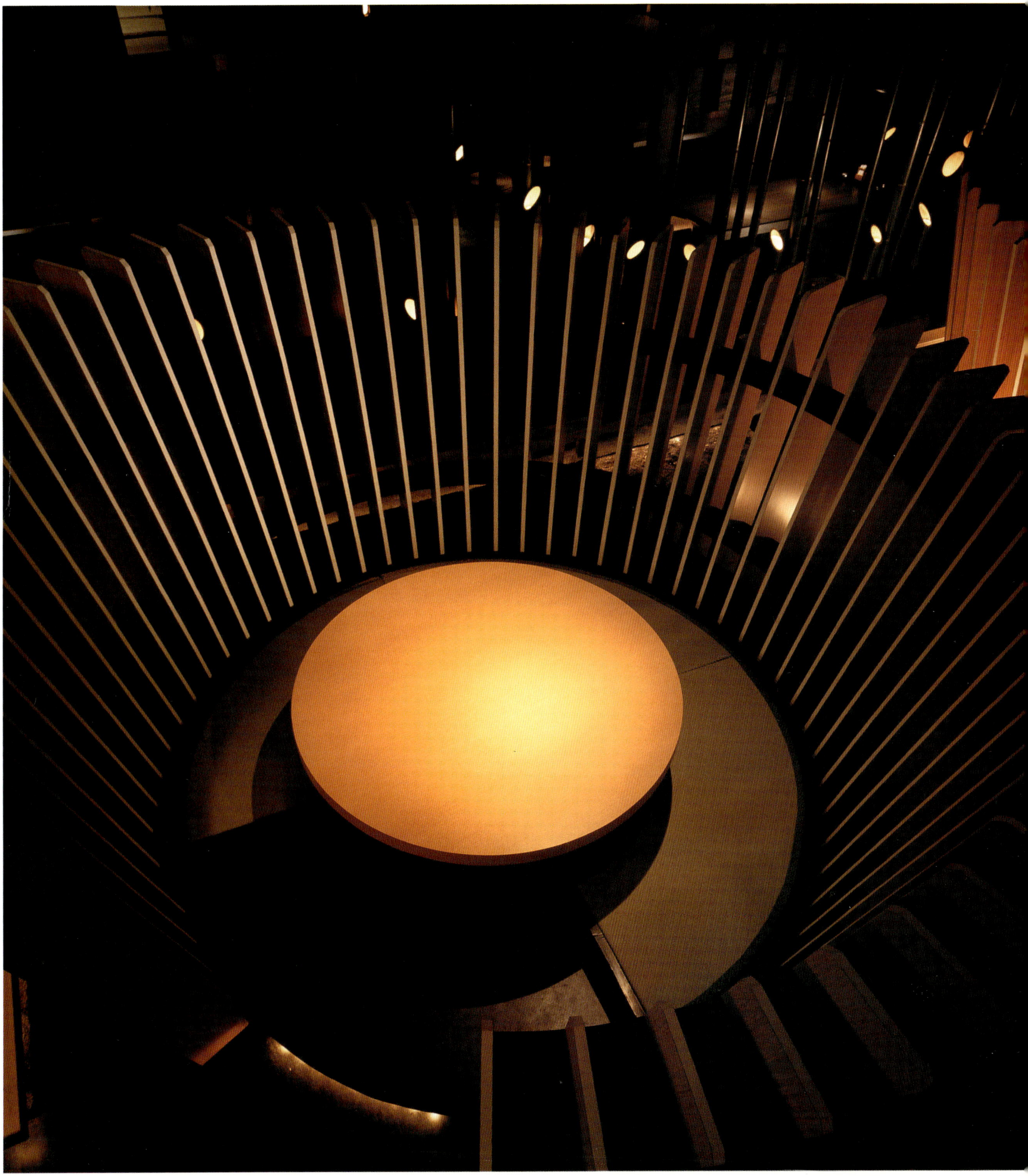

FIRST FLOOR

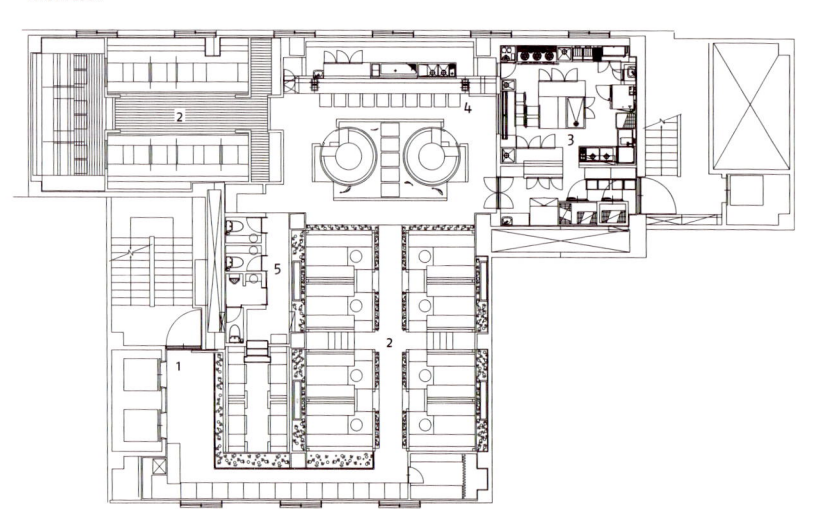

SECOND FLOOR

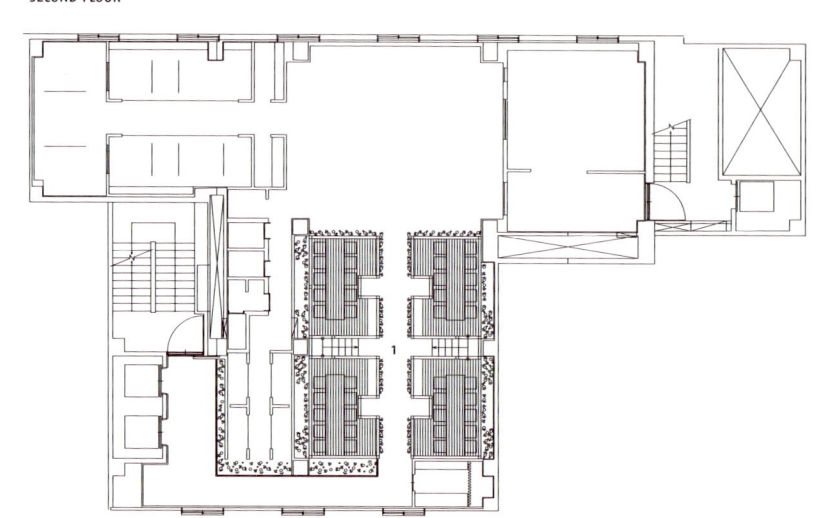

FIRST FLOOR
1 entrance
2 dining area
3 kitchen
4 bar
5 washroom

SECOND FLOOR
1 dining area

今宵、かぐや姫を誘うための魅惑の空間。

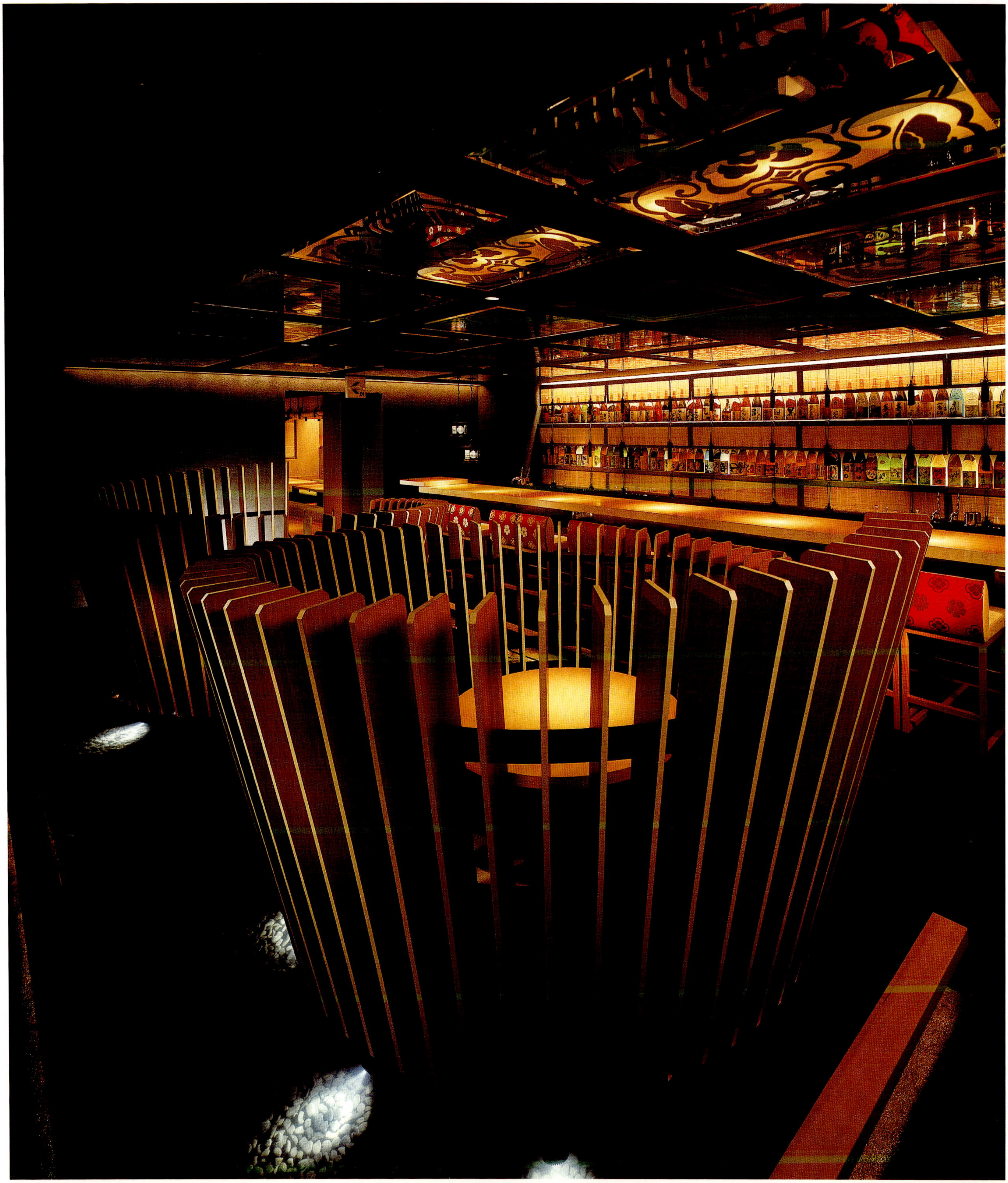

東京

竹取百物語

Taketori 100 Monogatari

The princess of the bamboo forest

Designer Katsunori Suzuki created this restaurant based on a famous tale from the early Heian Period. Japanese children are as familiar with the story as German children are with Hansel and Gretel. Taketori Monogatari (The Tale of the Bamboo Cutter), also known as Kaguyahime (Princess Kaguya), describes an old man who finds a baby girl inside a glowing bamboo tree. He and his wife decide to raise the child as their own. She grows up to be a beautiful young lady.

Different rooms of the restaurant resemble different stages of the child's life. One room looks like the bamboo forest where Princess Kaguya was found; the wall of another room is plastered to depict craters of the moon, where she claims she was born and will later return to.

The restaurant's main room resembles the place where Princess Kaguya grows up. Here Suzuki creatively added Japanese features that are visually very effective. Two round seating areas in the centre of the restaurant are built above a pond with real koi (carp). Suzuki said that when the restaurant opened, they were tiny but have grown into rather big fishes since then. The wood planks around the seats are designed in the image of Japanese fans. Since the ceiling of the room was very low, Suzuki used mirrors with patterns from the Heian period to visually enhance the space. He also used the fabric for real obi (Japanese kimono belts) to line the backing of the stools at the counter. The fabric's lucent red adds a splash of colour to the natural tone of the interior.

PHOTOGRAPHY	Masahiro Ishibashi
DESIGNER	Zoukei Syudan Co.,Ltd.
DESIGN TEAM	Yusaku Kaneshiro, Miho Umeda
CONTRACTOR	Kadoshika Food System
ADDRESS	Kashimada-Thousand Mall 2F, 201 Shin-Tsukakoshi, Saiwai-ku, Kawasaki City, Kanagawa 212-0027
PHONE	+81 (0) 4 4522 4610
AREA	264 m²
SEATING	151 seats
COMPLETED	2004

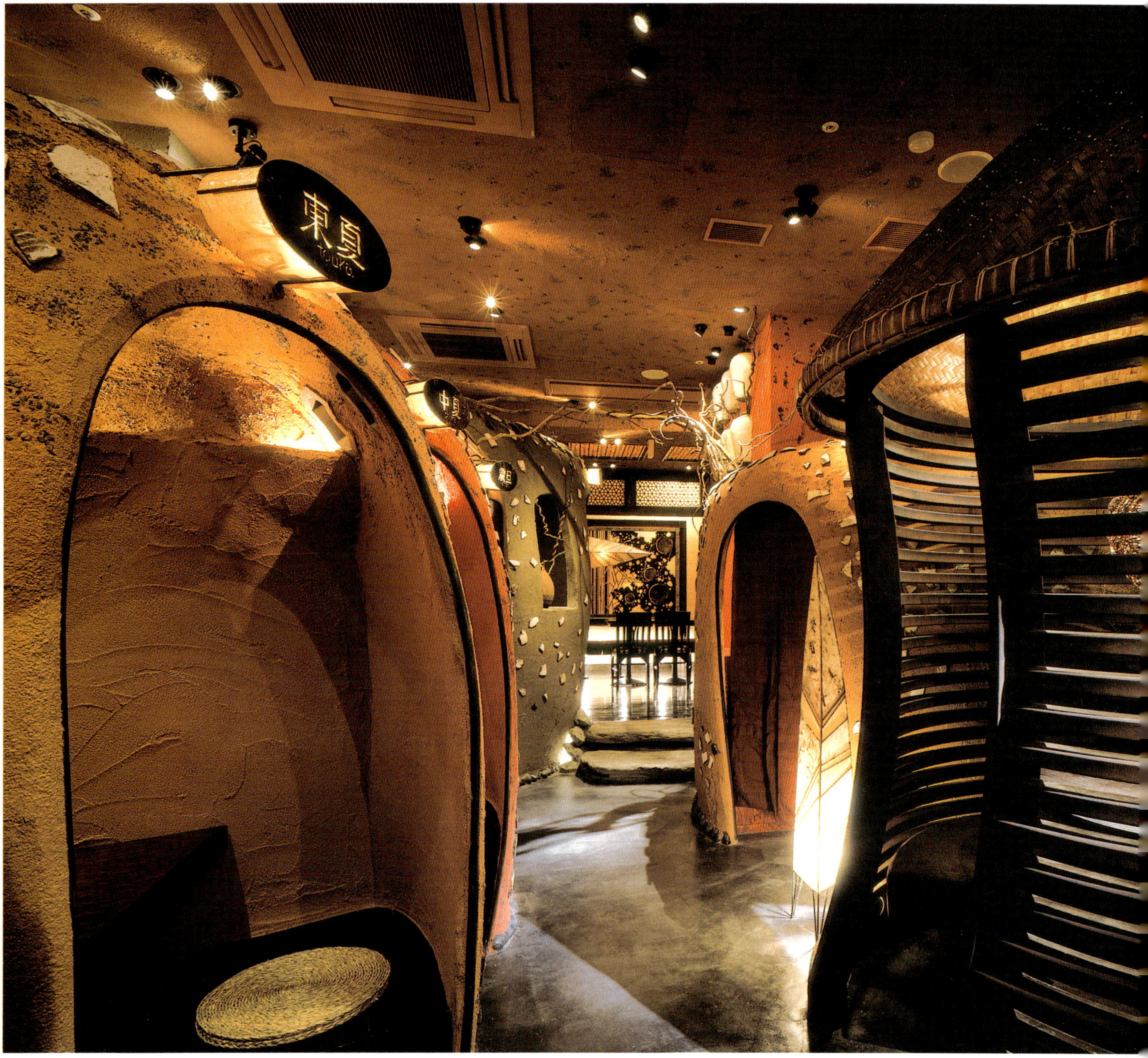
東夏

命を思わす造形が、やすらぎを醸す場所。

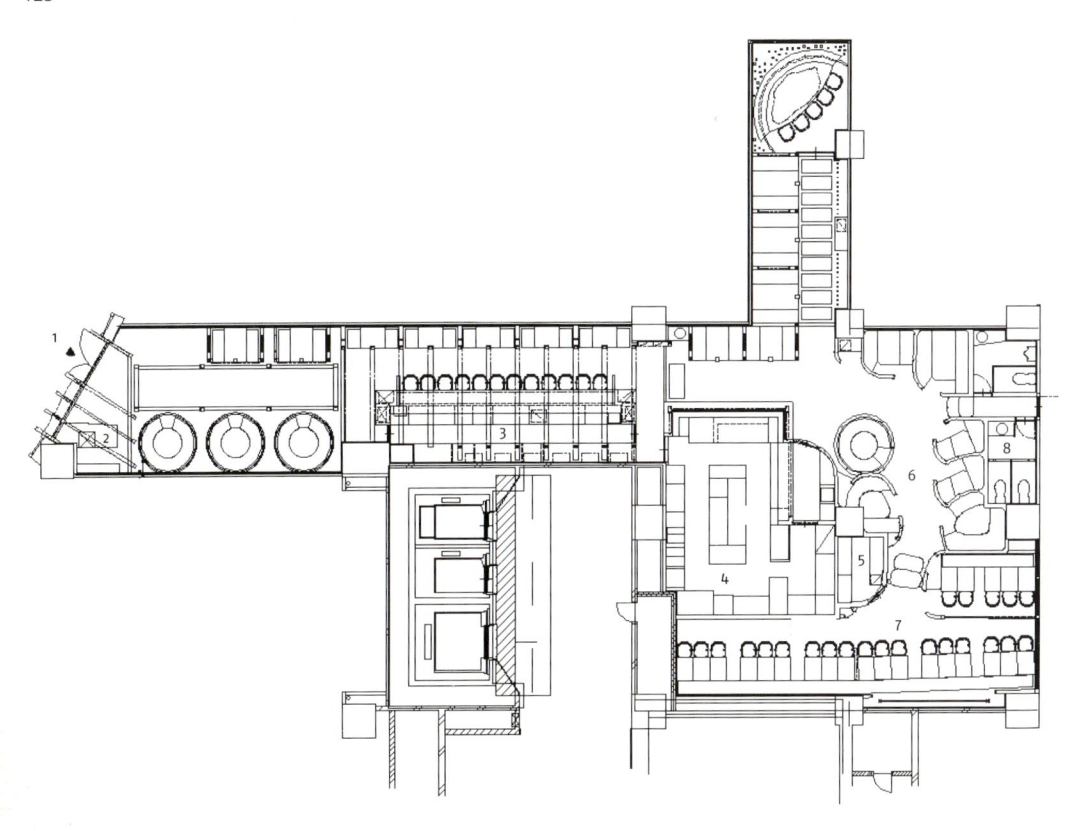

FLOORPLAN

1 entrance
2 cashier
3 bar
4 kitchen
5 staff room
6 dining area
7 party room
8 washroom

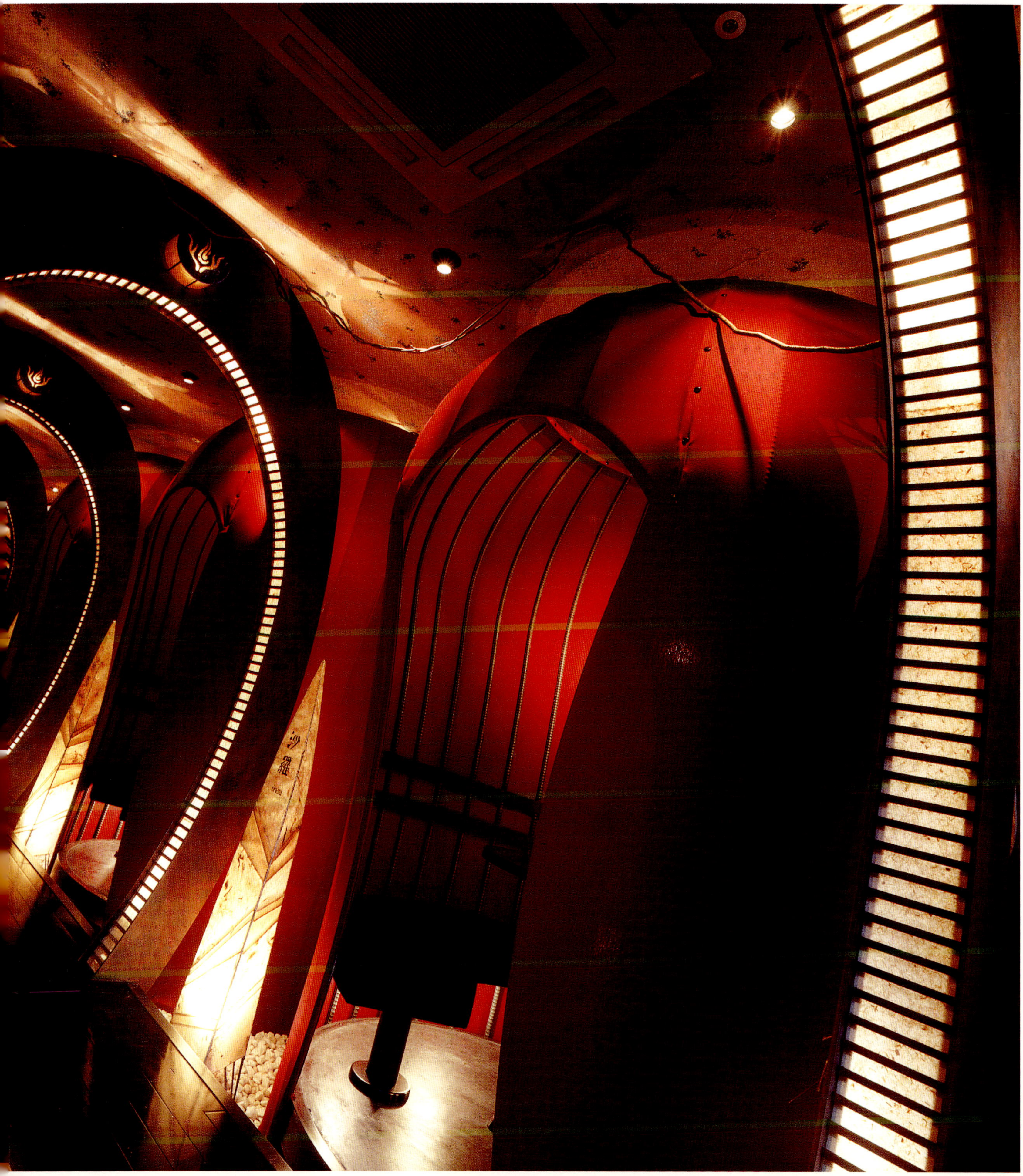

沙羅
sara

川崎

角鹿

Kadoshika

Finding respite in organic design

Entering the Chinese restaurant through the hallway is already an aesthetic experience. A wooden footbridge over pebble flooring leads into the dining area. Rectangular glass windows integrated with the timberwork reveal stone lamps that softly illuminate the scene from below. Several archways that emit subtle light loom over the catwalk. On the wall to the left, there are half-embedded Chinese liquor flasks surrounded by real twigs. Together with actual bins and pebbles, these reflect designer Yusaku Kaneshiro's preference for the use of authentic materials for a natural look and feel.

Kadoshika's highlights are the private booths that are characteristic of Kaneshiro's designs. In Japan where apartments are usually tiny and opportunities for a quiet retreat are few, these private booths allow couples or small groups to dine in a homely, private atmosphere. The steel scaffold constructions covered with red tent fabric are particularly outstanding, covered only externally to leave the construction visible inside. The other comb-shaped cubicles that are decorated on the outside with earthy colours and real liquor flask shards also invite visitors to spend a relaxing time within.

The bar area stands out through its very individualistic lightning. Futuristic steel constructions that are illuminated from the inside surround the counter on the front and at the top. Real Japanese Washi paper is used as the interior lining of the steel and acrylic structure, creating an exceptional lighting effect.

PHOTOGRAPHY	Ellen Nepilly
DESIGNER	Fantastic Design Works
DESIGN TEAM	Katsunori Suzuki
CONTRACTOR	Diamond Dining Inc.
ADDRESS	Fujikyu Bldg. East Bldg. No.3 B1F, 2-16-8, Minami-Ikebukuro, Toshima- ku, Tokyo 171-0022
PHONE	+81 (0) 3 3985 2193
AREA	166 m²
SEATING	98 seats
COMPLETED	2005

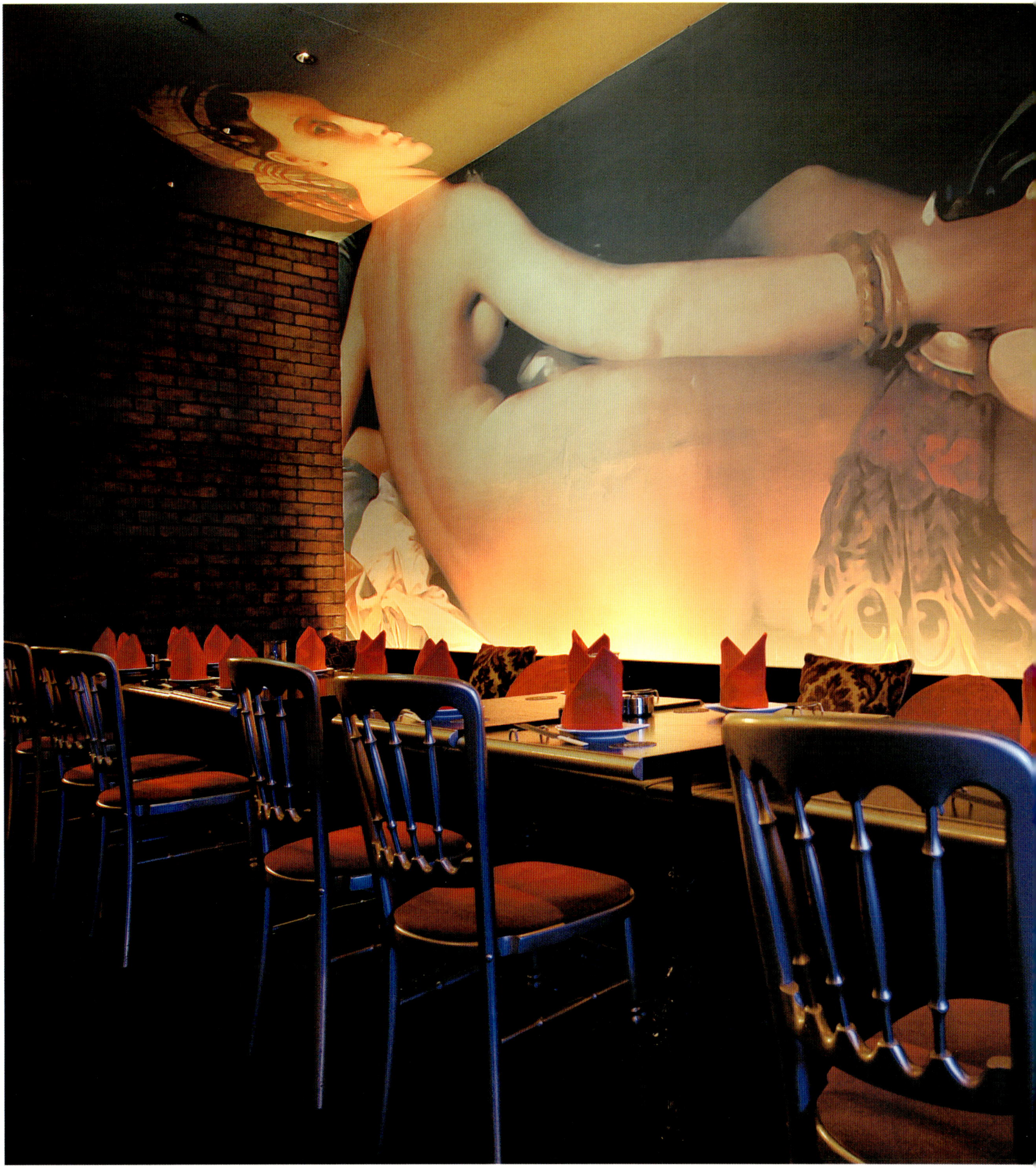

欧州の絢爛を濃密に封じ込めた煌めきの箱。

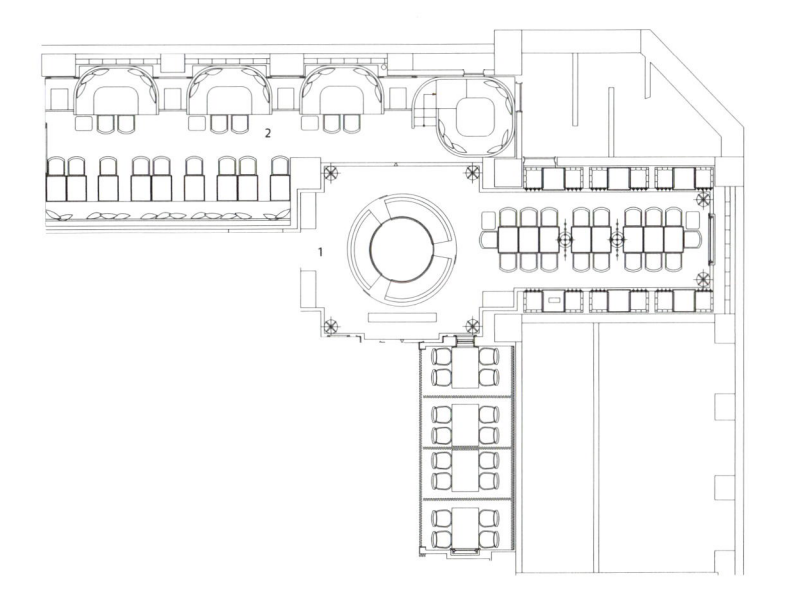

FLOORPLAN

1 entrance
2 dining area

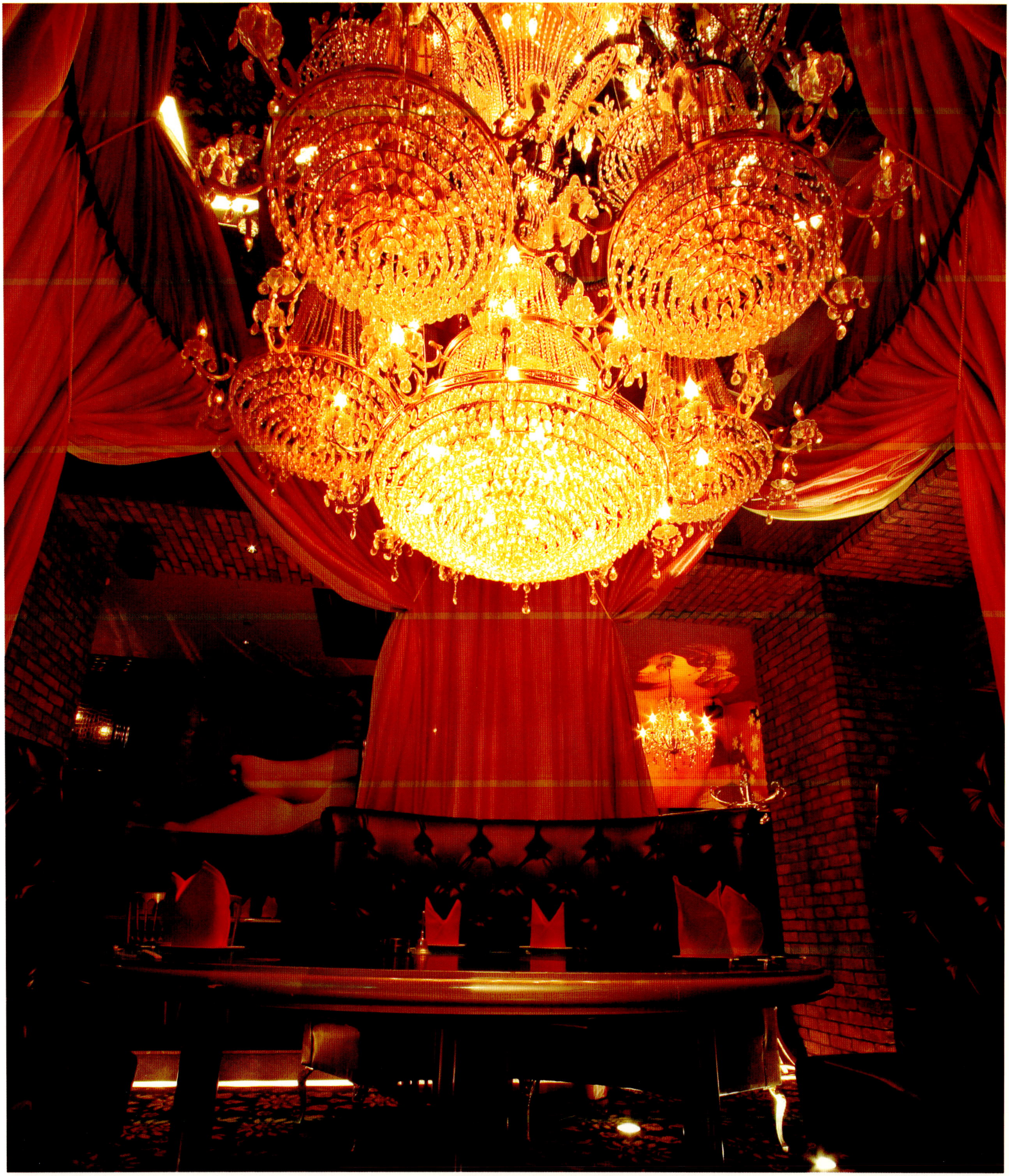

東京

オペラハウスの魔法使い

The Wizard of the Opera
The phantom of the opera descends on the Louvre

Years ago, when designer Katsunori Suzuki visited Paris, he was very much impressed by the Louvre. The ceiling's architecture and drawings, as well as Jean-Auguste-Dominique Ingres' oil painting "La Grande Odalisque", left the deepest impressions in his mind.

Suzuki used these impressions and integrated them into the interior of this Tokyo restaurant. The two enlargements of "La Grande Odalisque" on wallpaper in one dining area virtually became the most impressive feature of this outstanding space. The ceiling of another room was modelled after the image of the Louvre's impressive ceiling. The stage of the film "The Phantom of the Opera" provided another source of inspiration. Motifs from the movie, such as masks decorating the walls, or ropes hanging from the ceiling, lent the interior a special touch. The film sets also inspired the seating area in the centre of the establishment, with its colossal chandeliers, comfortable rounded benches and gigantic surrounding curtains. With the indirect illumination on the floor, the surreal illusion that The Wizard of the Opera offers is simply marvellous.

PHOTOGRAPHY	Hirokazu Matsuoka
DESIGNER	calm.design co., ltd.
DESIGN TEAM	Takuya Kanazawa
CONTRACTOR	Diamond Dining
ADDRESS	Seno Bldg. 5F, 3-18-4 Shinjuku, Sinjuku-ku, Tokyo 160-0022
PHONE	+81 (0) 3 3226 2855
AREA	275 m²
SEATING	160 seats, 17 private rooms
COMPLETED	2005

118

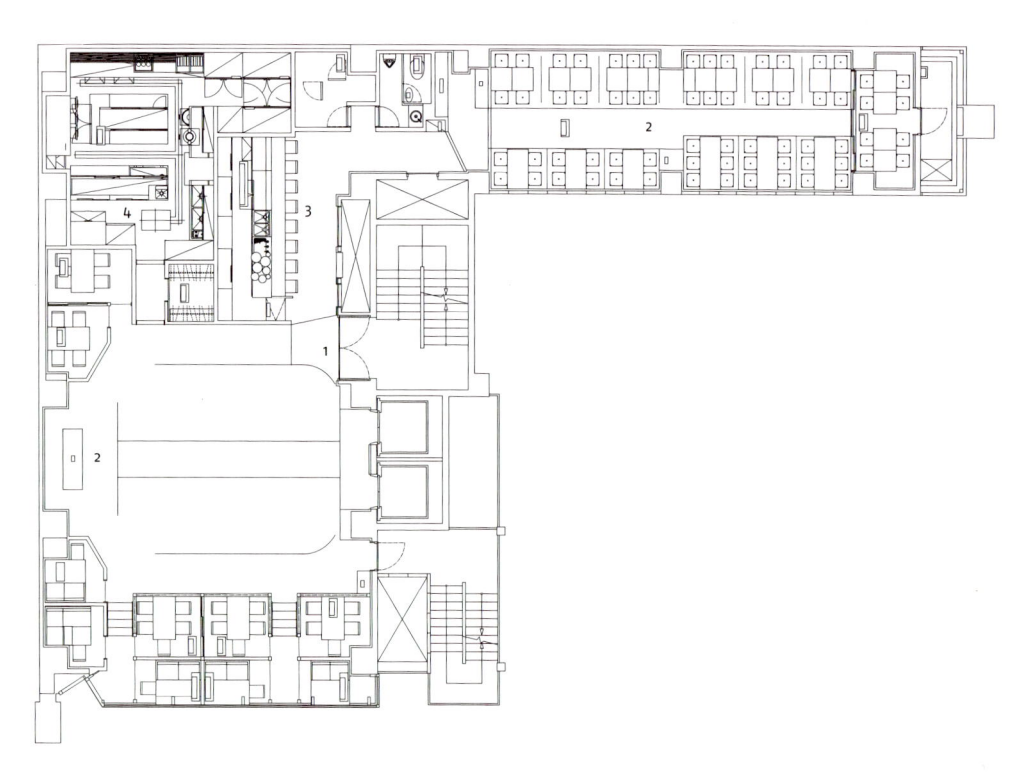

FLOORPLAN
1 entrance
2 dining area
3 bar
4 kitchen

花のある空間に生まれる、華のある時間。

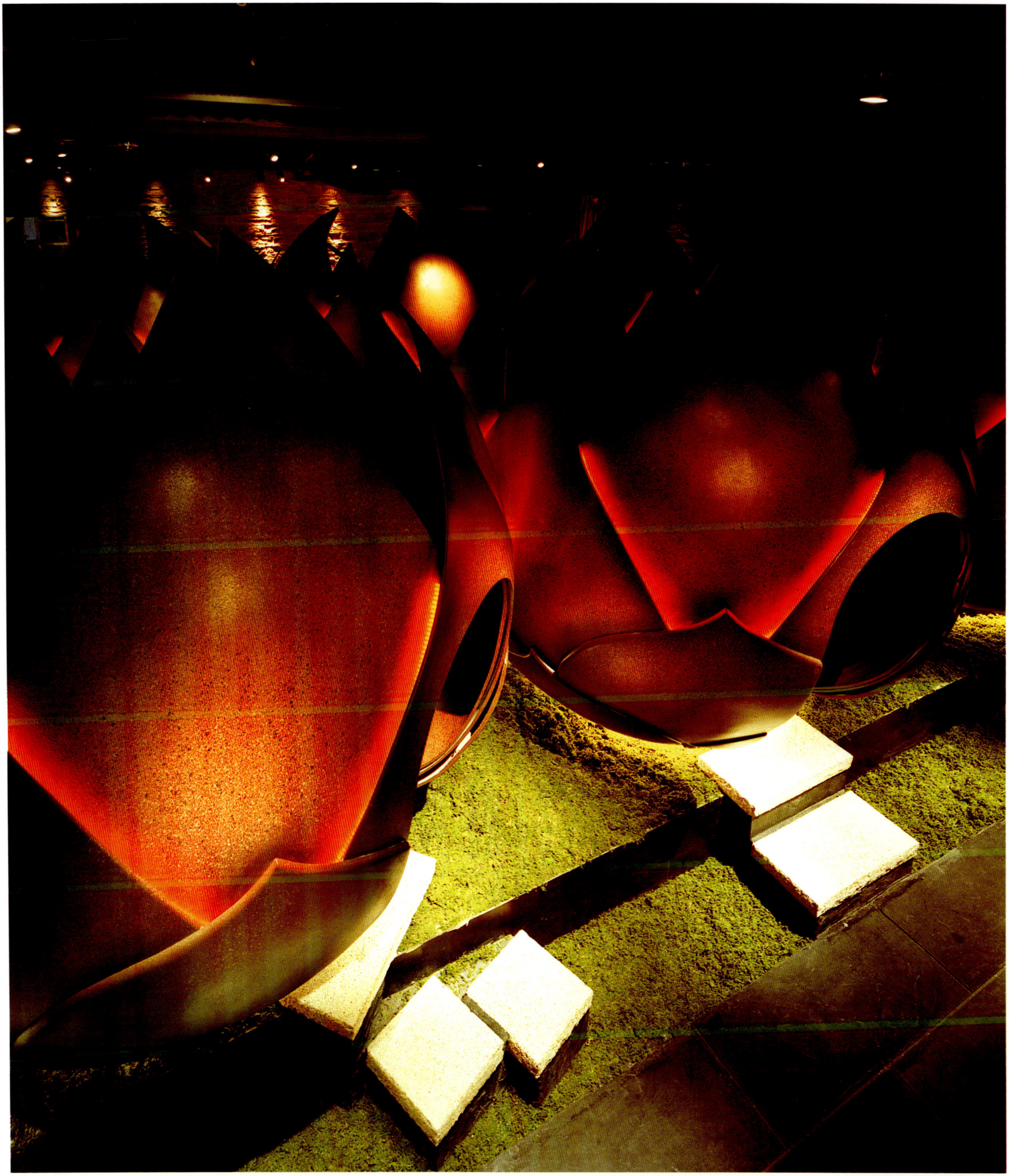

Tsubomi

つぼみ

Privacy amidst blooming flowers

It could be the stage of a fantasy film. When guests exit from Tsubomi's elevator, many are surprised by what they walk into. On both sides of the stone-paved aisle, private dining booths resembling gigantic flower buds welcome the diners. White stepping-stones on the meadow-like flooring lead into small openings, where one can walk through the beautifully illuminated petals of the flower buds. Sitting around a small table inside the buds, small groups can dine, drink and talk while sitting close to each other, without anyone feeling left out.

Larger groups or those who prefer a bigger space can bypass this man-made garden to another section that is designed to look like a red-light district from the Edo Period. The blinds in these rooms can be opened or closed, depending on how much privacy the parties prefer. Through the blinds, guests can overlook the flower buds or Tsubomi. Other rooms, where couples can enjoy conversations in privacy, offer views overlooking the Shinjuku night scene. For large parties or banquets, Tsubomi offers the Flower Gallery, where the aura of different flowers like lotus, iris, and Chinese bellflower is integrated together. The Flower Gallery can accommodate up to 80 persons.

PHOTOGRAPHY	Masahiro Ishibashi
DESIGNER	Zoukei Syudan Co., Ltd.
DESIGN TEAM	Yusaku Kaneshiro, Micho Umeda
CONTRACTOR	Midori-Syoji
ADDRESS	Higashi 2 Gou-kan B1F, Hujihisa Bldg., 1-20-3 Minami-Ikebukuro, Toshima-ku, Tokyo 171-0022
PHONE	+81 (0) 3 5960 9293
AREA	179 m²
SEATING	129 seats
COMPLETED	2003

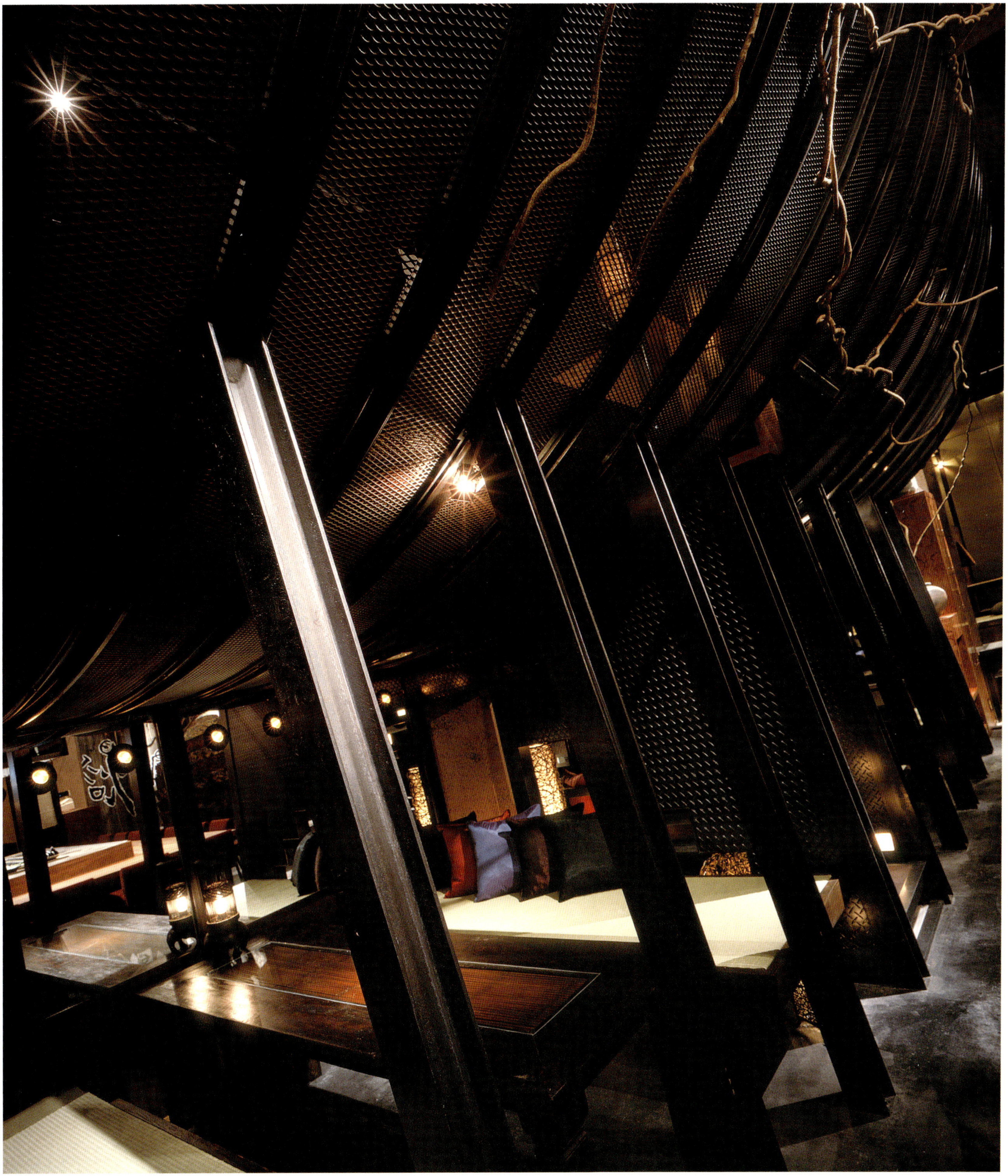

FLOORPLAN

1   entrance
2   cashier
3   dining area
4   kitchen
5   tatami room
6   washroom

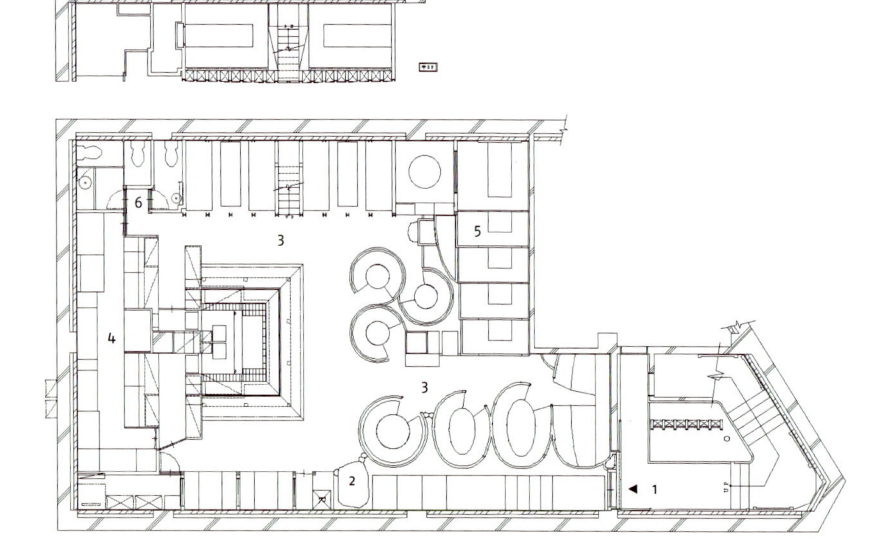

木と鉄と火が創造する、優しく柔軟な空間。

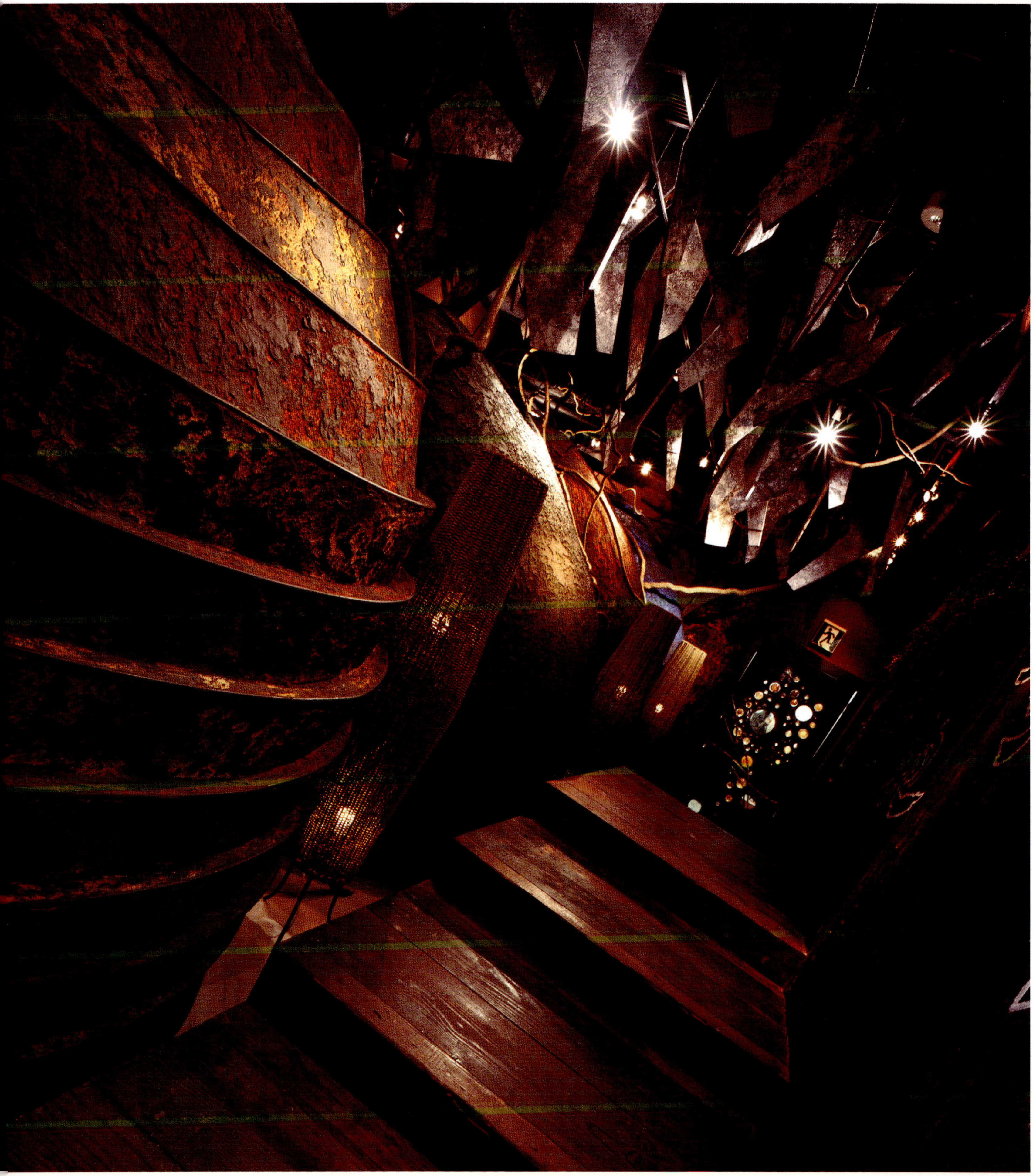

東京

炉ぶた屋

Robutaya

Taking Japanese grill dining a few steps further

The distinctly coloured private booths are one of the most outstanding features of this restaurant. They have cocoon-like shapes with insides that are reminiscent of caves. The booths are ideal for guests who seek privacy and seclusion. Designer Yusaku Kaneshiro even thought of integrating a circular-shaped hole in the ceiling as a ventilation funnel for cigarette smoke. The booth design was modelled after a building that Kaneshiro saw on a trip to London. The impressive decoration of the ceiling resembles a huge glass cullet hanging overhead. But guests need not worry - the material from which these objects are made is very light.

Another interesting area of this establishment is its room with Tatami mats made from Japanese raw materials. This room is rather long and narrow and structured like a staircase, with each step functioning as a seating area. The mats serve not only as flooring to sit upon but also as walls and ceilings. The seats at different levels add to the enjoyable dining experience in Robutaya. The name Robutaya is derived from wordplay on the Japanese word for pig, "buta" and "robataya", which refers to traditional Japanese restaurant grills.

Call buttons are installed at the dining tables, which guests can use whenever they want another drink or something more to eat. Unlike the tardy service one may experience in some countries, Japanese waiters and waitresses are always at the table in no time to take the order. It is both the extraordinary design and service that makes for a complete dining experience.

PHOTOGRAPHER	Hiroshi Tsujitani (Nacasa & Partners Inc.)
DESIGNER	Bayleaf Inc. & Descartes Inc.
DESIGN TEAM	Taro Maeda, Katsuhiko Yamamoto, Takumi Sato
CONTRACTOR	Sun Royal Co., Ltd.
ADDRESS	Ice Omiya Bldg. B1-B2 1-60 Nakacho, Omiya-ku Saitama City, Saitama 330-0845
PHONE	+81 (0) 4 8645 1919
AREA	226 m²
SEATING	92 seats
COMPLETED	2005

BASEMENT

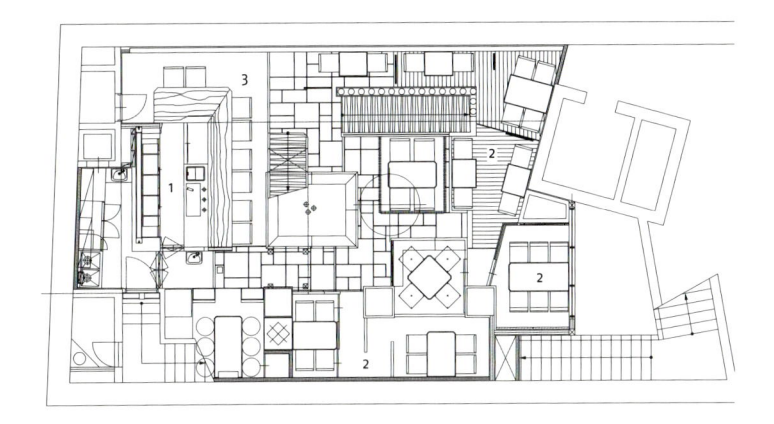

FIRST FLOOR

SECOND FLOOR

BASEMENT
1 counter
2 dining area
3 bar

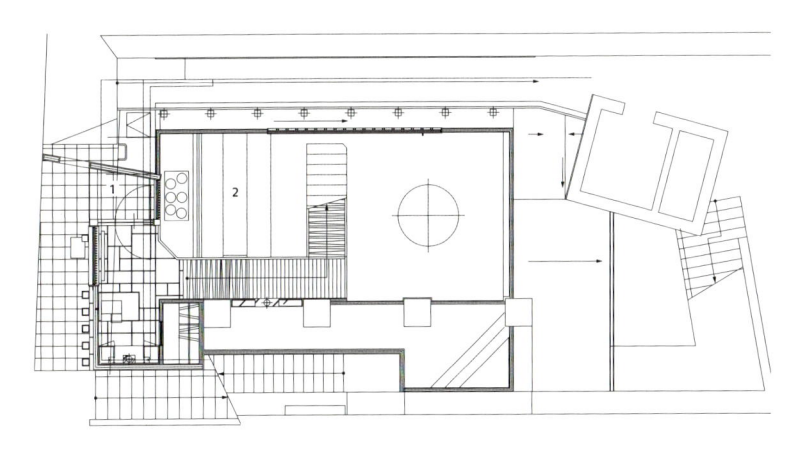

FIRST FLOOR
1 entrance
2 kitchen

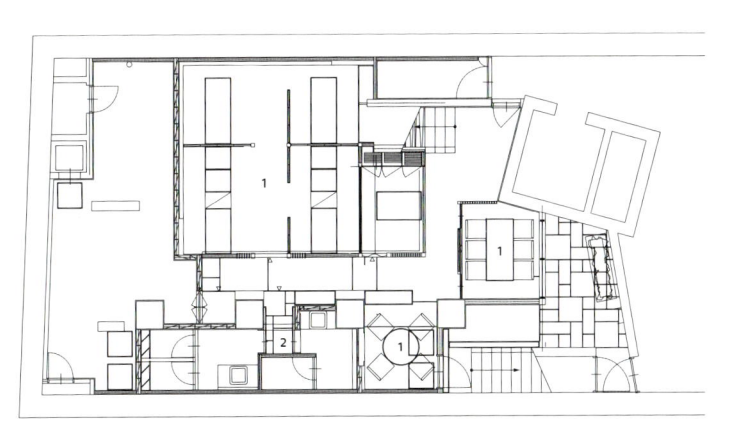

SECOND FLOOR
1 dining area
2 washroom

和の持つ繊細な線と質感、そして粋なはからい。

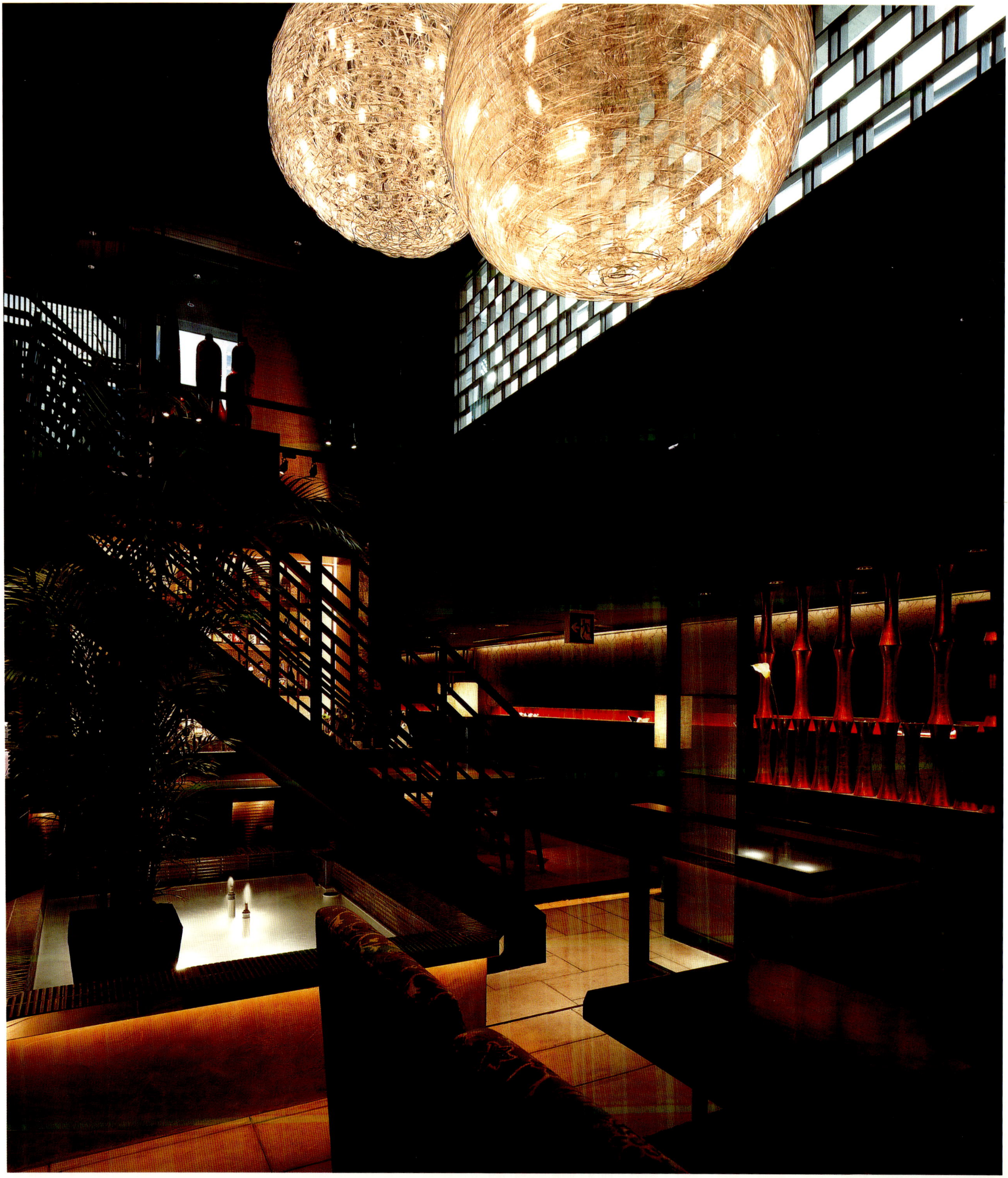

埼玉

Ikki

一粋

Modern installations meshing with Oriental art

The second character of the restaurant's Japanese name means good-looking, stylish, or chic – and so is its interior. The design concept is a tasteful and trendy blend of oriental and modern design.

The high ceiling of about seven metres made it difficult to fill the space tastefully and prevent it from appearing too large and empty. Even the huge wire mesh lamps with a diameter of about 80 cm do not look out of proportion; in fact they fill the space just perfectly. It is ingenious how such attractive lamps can be crafted from ordinary wire mesh enhanced with illumination. In contrast to the dark tones of the wood, they are indeed eyecatching. Then there are the scarlet lacquer flower vases imported from Bangkok, some stacked above each other like pillars, combined with a luminous red lining in the wall, which stand out and add a touch of oriental elegance to the interior. The partitions made of wood and stainless steel wire mesh are similarly outstanding, and given the tasteful composition of that floor's design, coupled with the relaxing image of the fountain, the space becomes more of a tastefully furnished modern living room than a restaurant.

Ascend the beautiful stairs that lean over the fountain, and emerge at the second level that sports modern Japanese design, where Japanese calligraphy artist Takako Mori drew an ink graphic on the spot for display.

PHOTOGRAPHY	Masahiro Ishibashi
DESIGNER	Zoukei Syudan Co., Ltd.
DESIGN TEAM	Yusaku Kaneshiro, Mitsuru Komatsuzaki
CONTRACTOR	Yasuke Foods
ADDRESS	52-16 Ishikawa-cho, Hakodate City, Hokkaido, 041-0802
PHONE	+81 (0) 1 3847 0102
AREA	322 m²
SEATING	144 seats
COMPLETED	2004

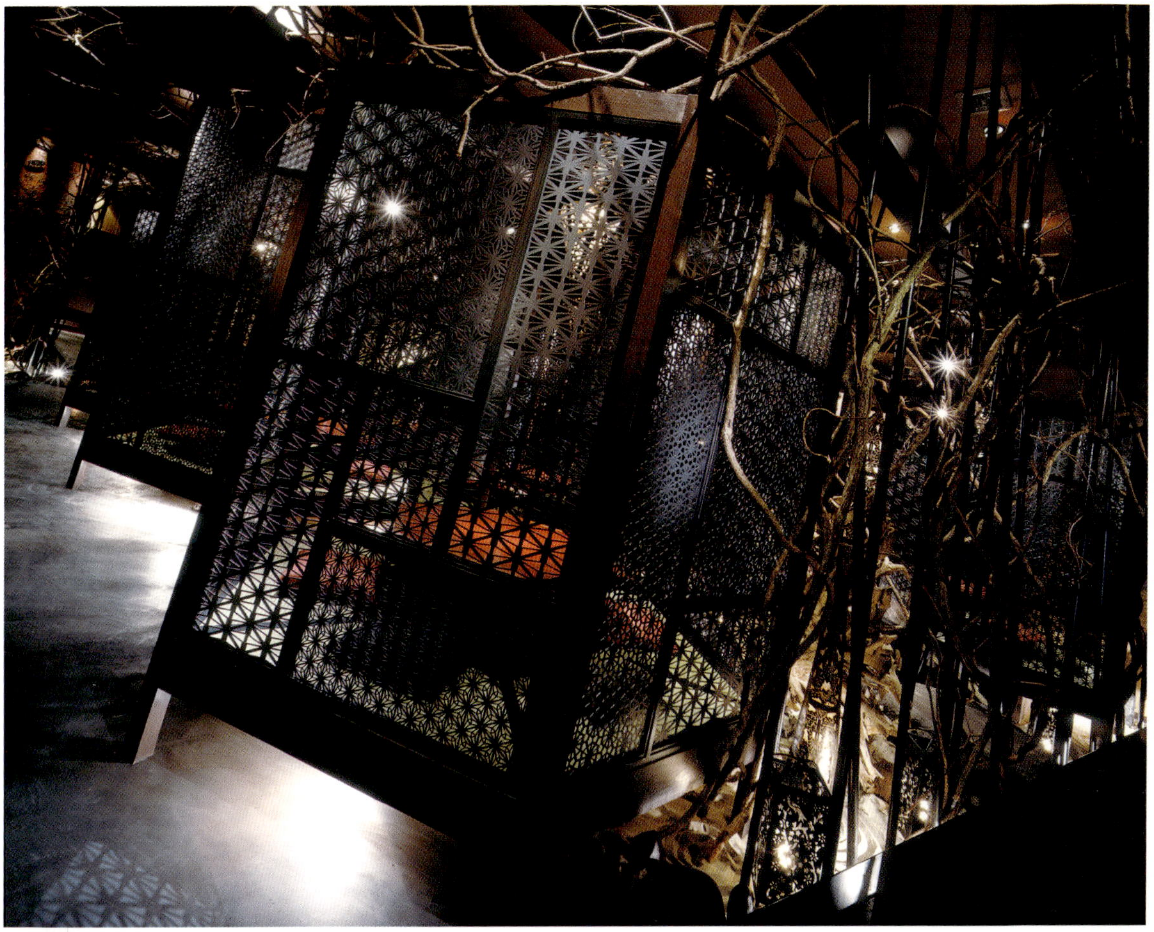

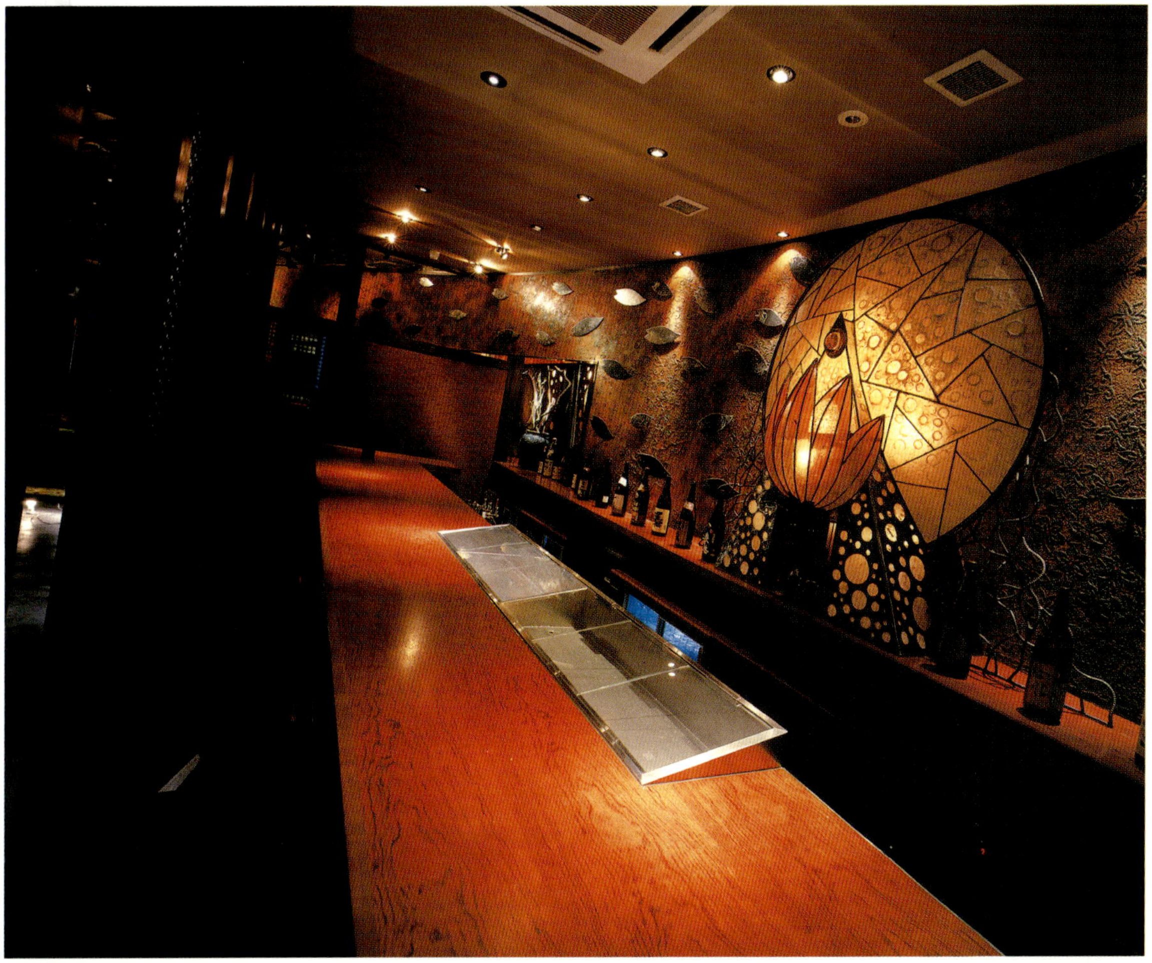

FIRST FLOOR
1 entrance
2 cashier
3 dining area
4 counter
5 bed seats
6 party room
7 kitchen
8 staff room
9 washroom

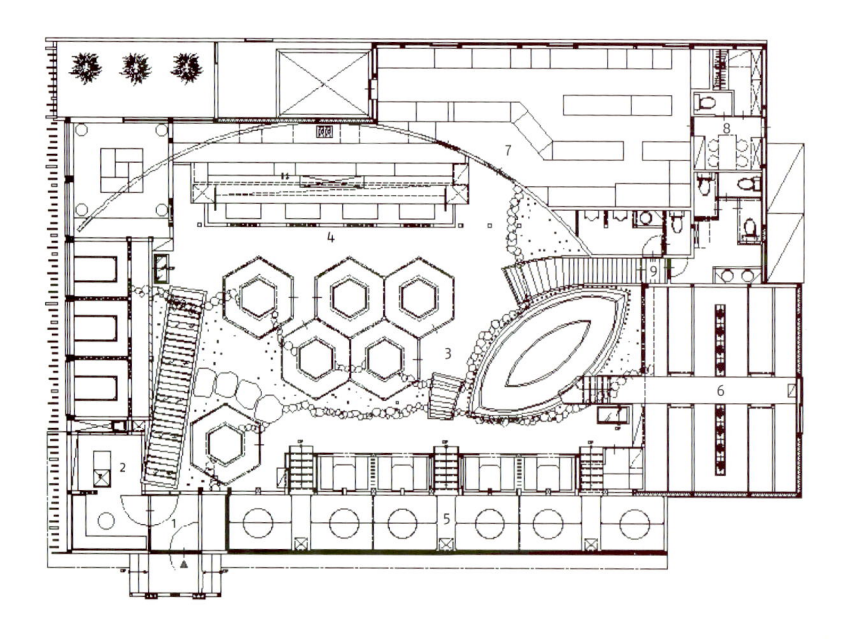

月に咲く華は、人に静謐の美を思わせる。

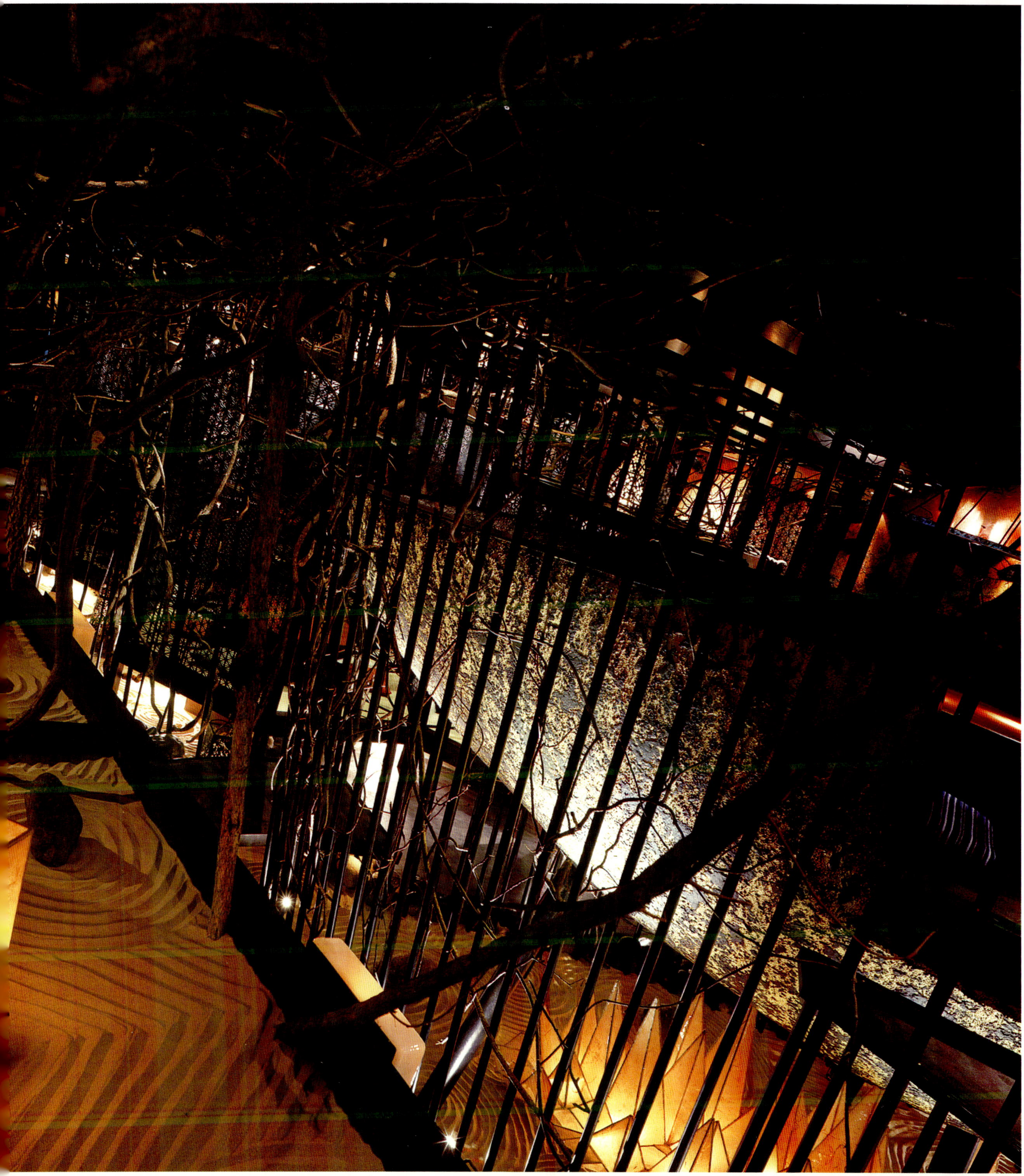

函館

Get' ska

Amidst nature's entwining fingers

Located on Japan's northernmost and second largest island Hokkaido, the exceptional building that houses this sushi restaurant looks from afar like a house in a forest overgrown with flanking plants. On the roof sits a huge half moon-shaped construction that could work as a glasshouse, catching the eye of passersby. Those who are allured by the promise of its warmly-lit exterior will not be disappointed when they enter, for the interior is even more striking. Designer Yusaku Kaneshiro and his team based their design on Japanese styles and enhanced it with fantasy structures and organic materials. Like the outside, twisted tree branches virtually overgrow across every structure of Get'ska's interior. Real stones, Zen-like sand garden patterns, and acrylic lamps of different shapes set interesting accents with warm aesthetic illumination.

The lower area is literally a garden with hexagonal booths at its centre. Inside, guests can dine sitting on Tatami mats in a completely relaxing atmosphere, as they enjoy their meal and watch the garden around them. If you walk along the path that encircles the garden, you can explore other exciting spaces, such as the half moon-shaped platform that looks like a ship floating in the air. This is surely the most intriguing visual feature of this dreamscape dining haven. Guests can enter it via a flight of stairs to sit in their own private lounge overlooking the whole interior of the restaurant, much like the luxurious feeling of looking down from a tribune in a grand theatre.

In another elevated section of the restaurant above the private dining rooms, Kaneshiro integrated pairs of mattresses with a round table in the centre to create a comfortable lounge section. Guests can observe the scenery lying down and if they get tired or drunk, they can just roll over and take a nap.

PHOTOGRAPHY	Shingi Miyamoto
DESIGNER	SOI
DESIGN TEAM	Akihiko Shoji
CONTRACTOR	Japan Chicken Food Service Ltd.
ADDRESS	Zain Ebisu Bldg. B1F 1-7-3 Ebisu-Nishi, Shibuya-ku, Tokyo 150-0021
PHONE	+ 81 (0) 3 5428 2288
AREA	238 m²
SEATING	120 seats
COMPLETED	2005

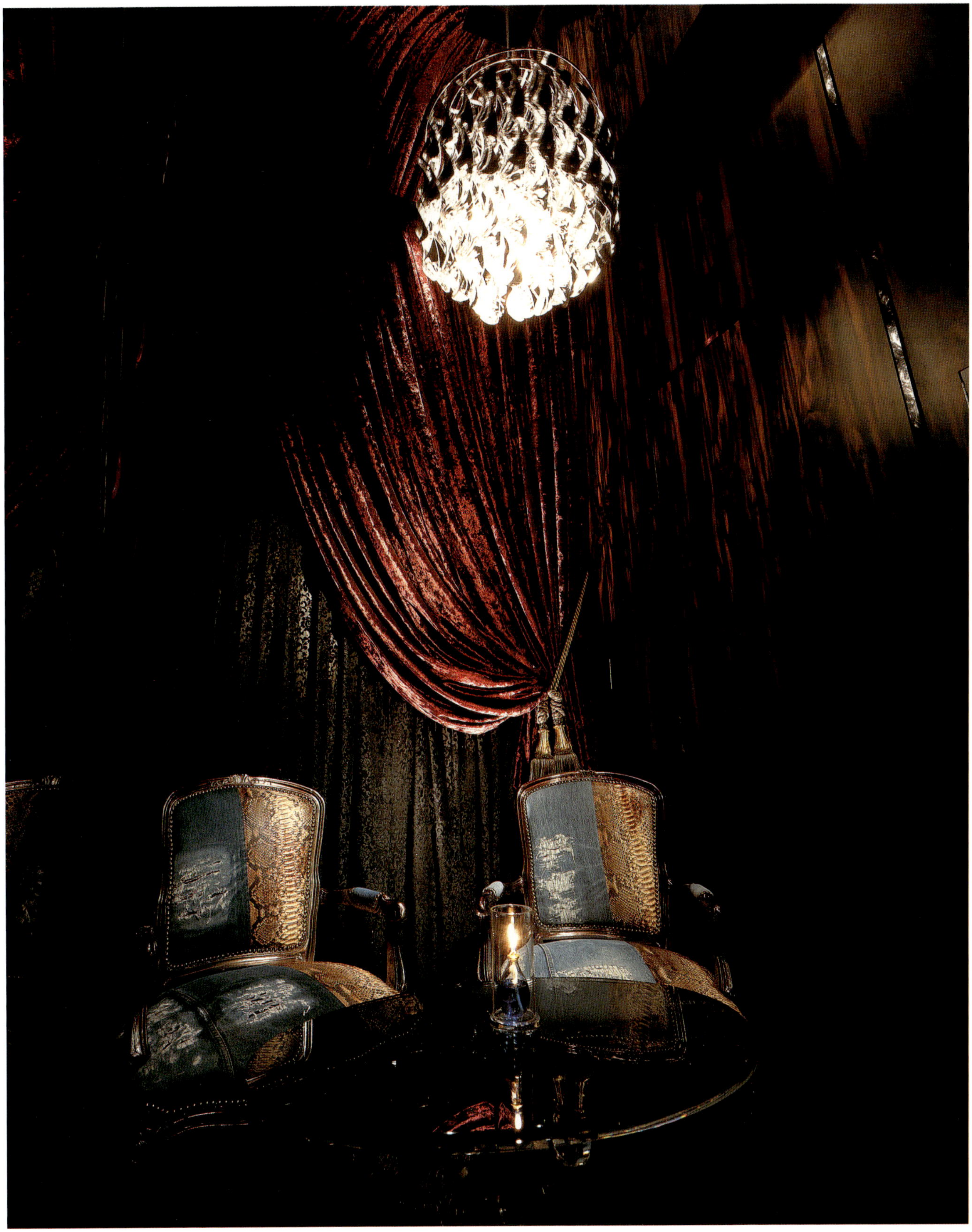
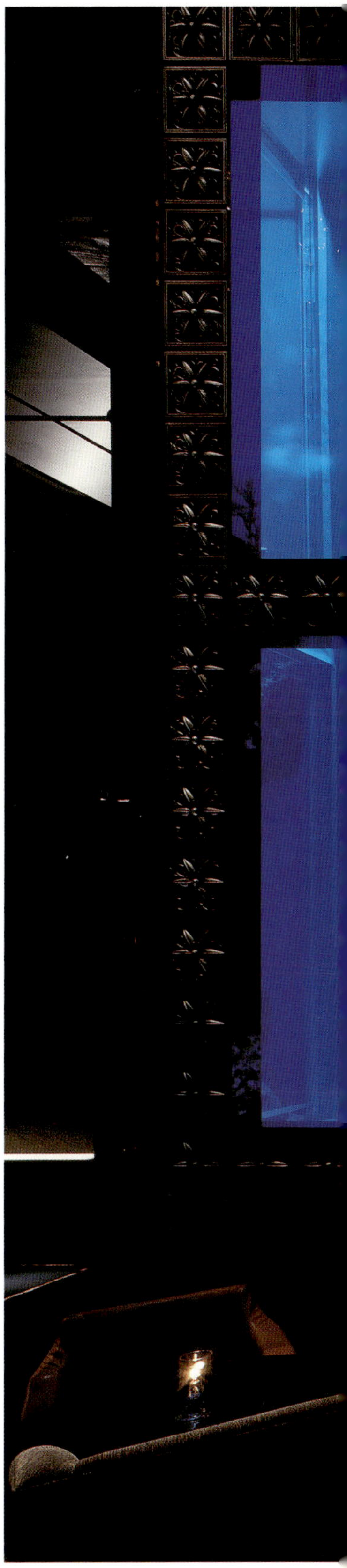

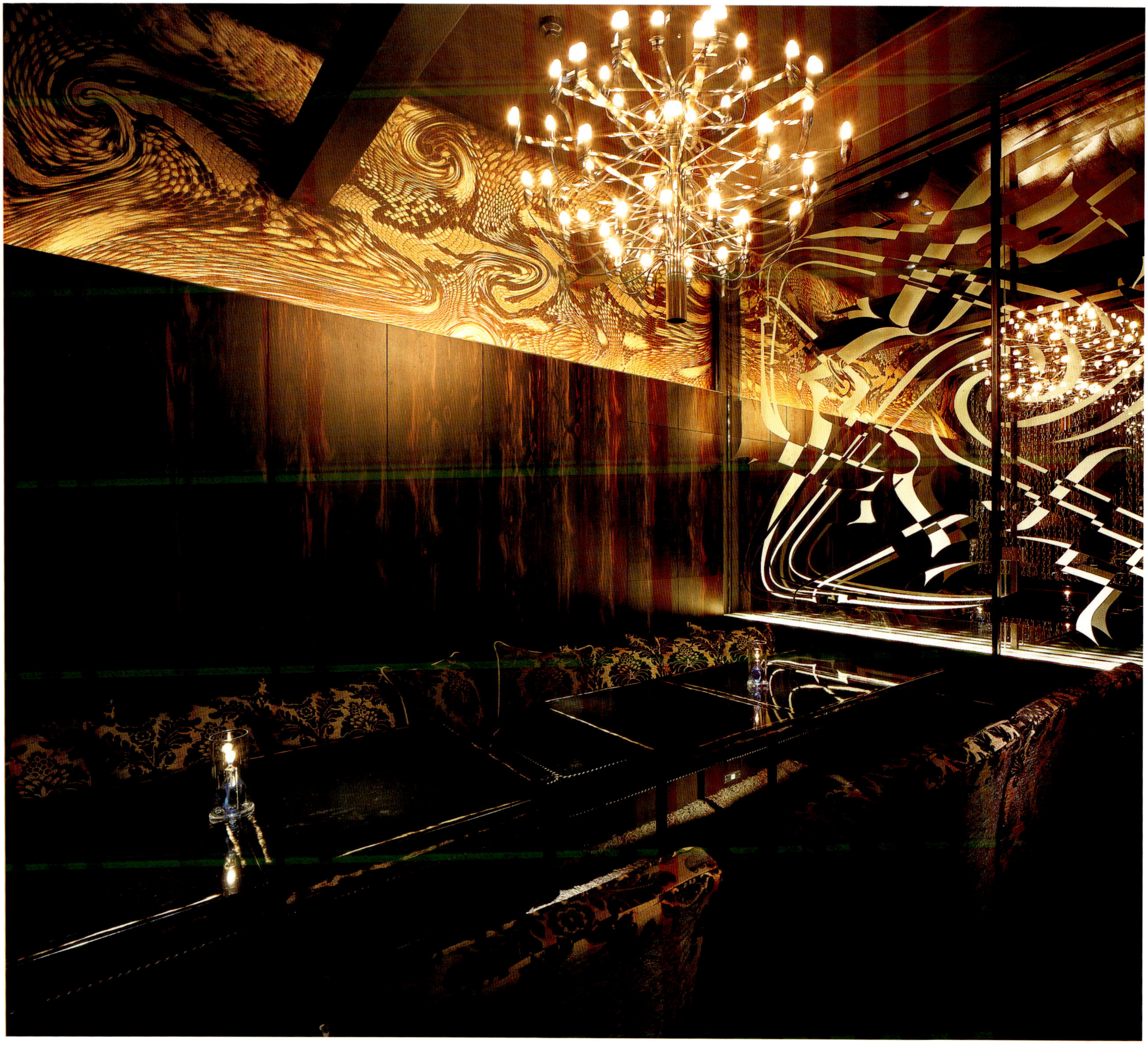

深海で楽しむ宴は、時間を忘れるお伽噺。

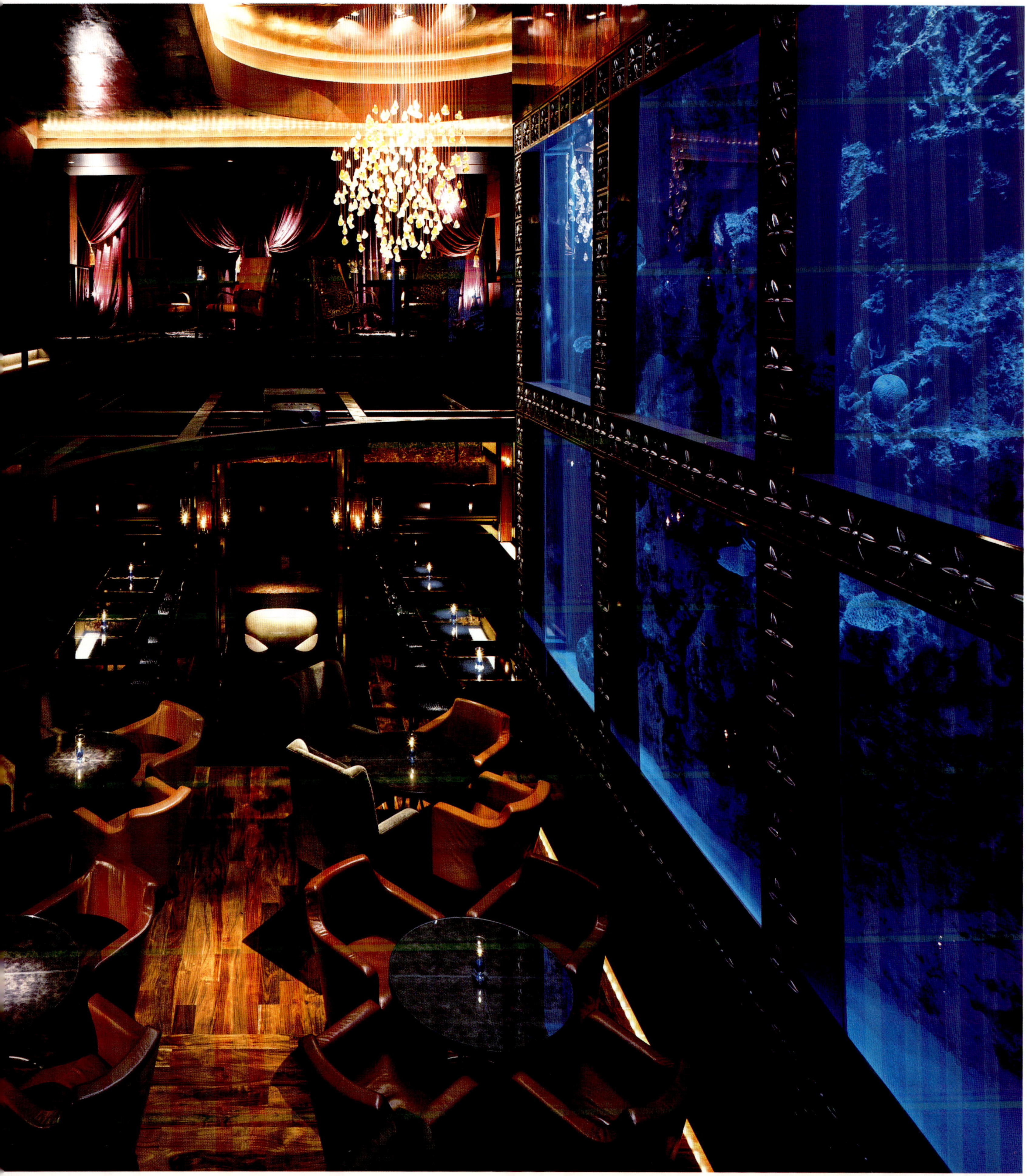

東京

ラグシス

Luxis

Dining in a mysterious underwater world

Looking from the entrance area down to the restaurant located in the basement, guests are mesmerised by the sight of a mysterious underwater world located inside a huge cave. The gigantic saltwater aquarium reaches up to the ceiling and fills about one-third of the wall, glowing with blue light that gives it an amazing aura.

Watching the various beautiful tropical fishes gliding around the huge rock in the tank, combined with the soothing effect of tranquil water, dining in Luxis is almost therapeutic, making its guests forget the outside world temporarily. However, to enjoy the view up close, guests have to pay a table surcharge, although the ambience makes it a worthwhile experience.

Dark wooden brown colours are combined with classic and stylish elements. Mirrors and glass with graphic patterns, damask curtains and chandeliers are skilfully blended into this luxurious and elegant setting. The chandeliers are particularly exceptional, with the most eye-catching chandelier looking like a shower of glass droplets frozen in time and space, hanging next to the aquarium.

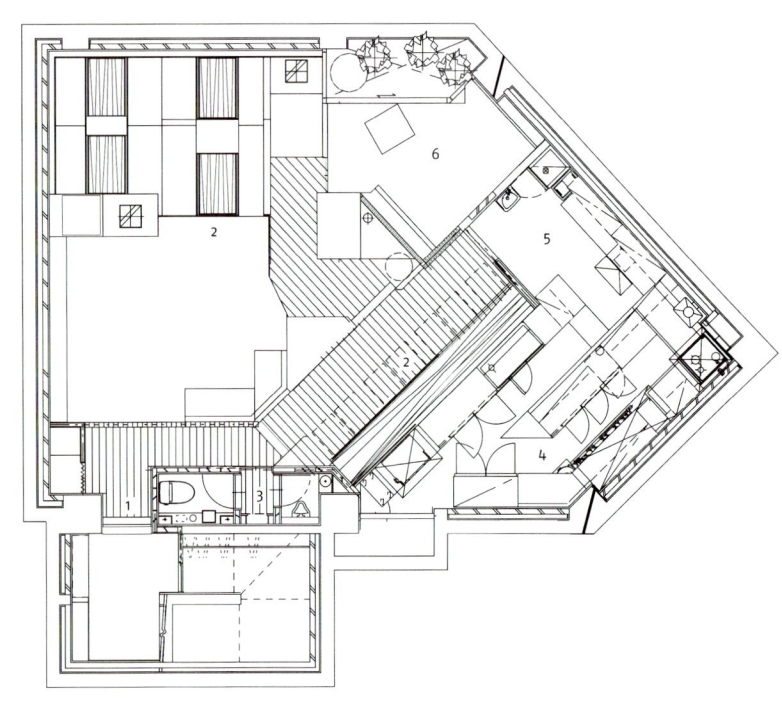

SECOND FLOOR
1 entrance
2 dining area
3 washroom
4 kitchen
5 pantry
6 lounge

風に舞い、漂い、浮かぶ美しさを愛でる夜に。

PHOTOGRAPHY	Hiroshi Tsujitani (Nacasa & Partners Inc.)
DESIGNER	Bayleaf Inc.
DESIGN TEAM	Taro Maeda
CONTRACTOR	7seas Global, Takahide Aisa
ADDRESS	DROP IN Daikanyama B1, 1-16-8 Ebisu-Nishi, Shibuya-ku, Tokyo 150-0021
PHONE	+81 (0) 3 5489 2510
AREA	97 m²
SEATING	50 seats
COMPLETED	2005

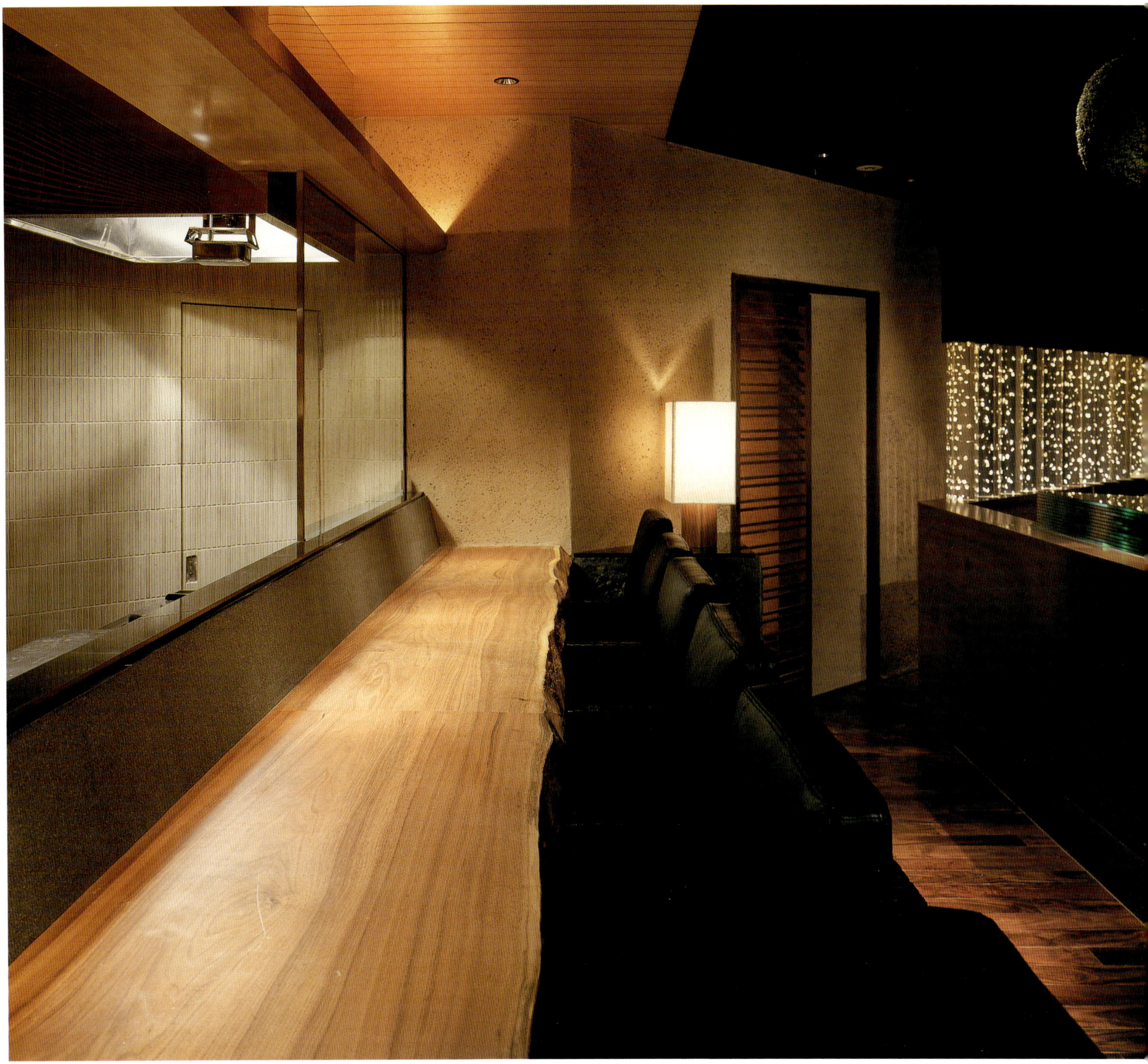

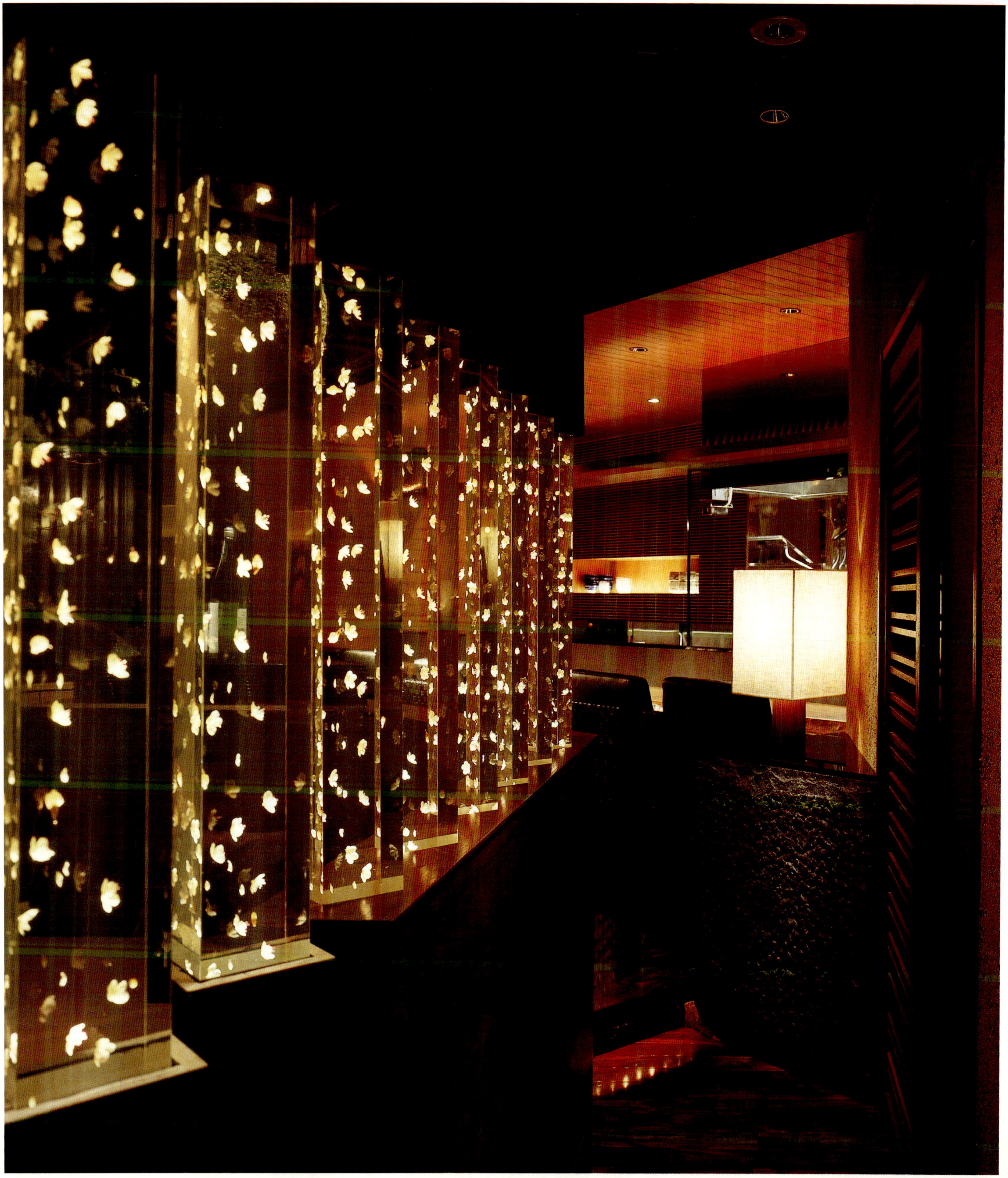

東京

ひらり

Hirari

Living dining kitchen

In Japan, LDK is an abbreviated description for a certain type of apartment. An LDK apartment includes a living room, a designated dining area, and a kitchen - although sometimes it might not be more than a tiny kitchenette. The number in front of LDK stands for the amount of extra rooms. For the interior of Hirari, designer Taro Maeda created an interior that is similar to a 3 LDK apartment – to make guests feel like they are in the private space of a comfortable apartment rather than a restaurant.

One room displays a western-style design with tables and chairs. Another resembles a Japanese room with a Tatami seating area, but with crevices in the floor where guests can comfortably rest their feet. The walls are lined with bamboo and Japanese Washi paper for a refreshing look. The third room's interior is like a living room and serves as a lounge from which guests can admire a small garden. By combining walnut wood with black leather sofas, adding striped carp and a glass chandelier, the end result is elegant and comfortable. Amidst all this, the most eye-catching piece is perhaps the big green sugidama ball that hangs from the ceiling. Sugidama balls are traditional Japanese decorations made from the sugi tree. Sake brewers used to hang it in front of their breweries to inform people when sake is available for sale. Hirari's sugidama ball comes from Maeda's friend, Azumamine Shuzo, who is also the owner of a sake brewery.

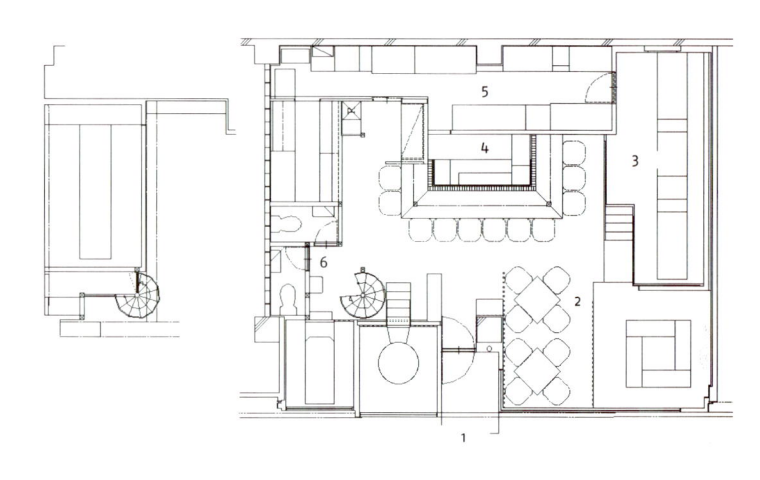

FLOORPLAN

1. entrance
2. dining area
3. arch room
4. grill counter
5. kitchen
6. washroom

PHOTOGRAPHY	Masahiro Ishibashi
DESIGNER	Zoukei Syudan Co., Ltd.
DESIGN TEAM	Yusaku Kaneshiro, Miho Umeda
CONTRACTOR	Ki・Raku・En
ADDRESS	Maruesu-Megane 1F, 1190 Ida-Machi, Ota City, Gunma 373-0851
PHONE	+81 (0) 2 7646 6007
AREA	99 m²
SEATING	75 seats
COMPLETED	2005

酒樽の中で酔いしれる、それは夢見る時間。

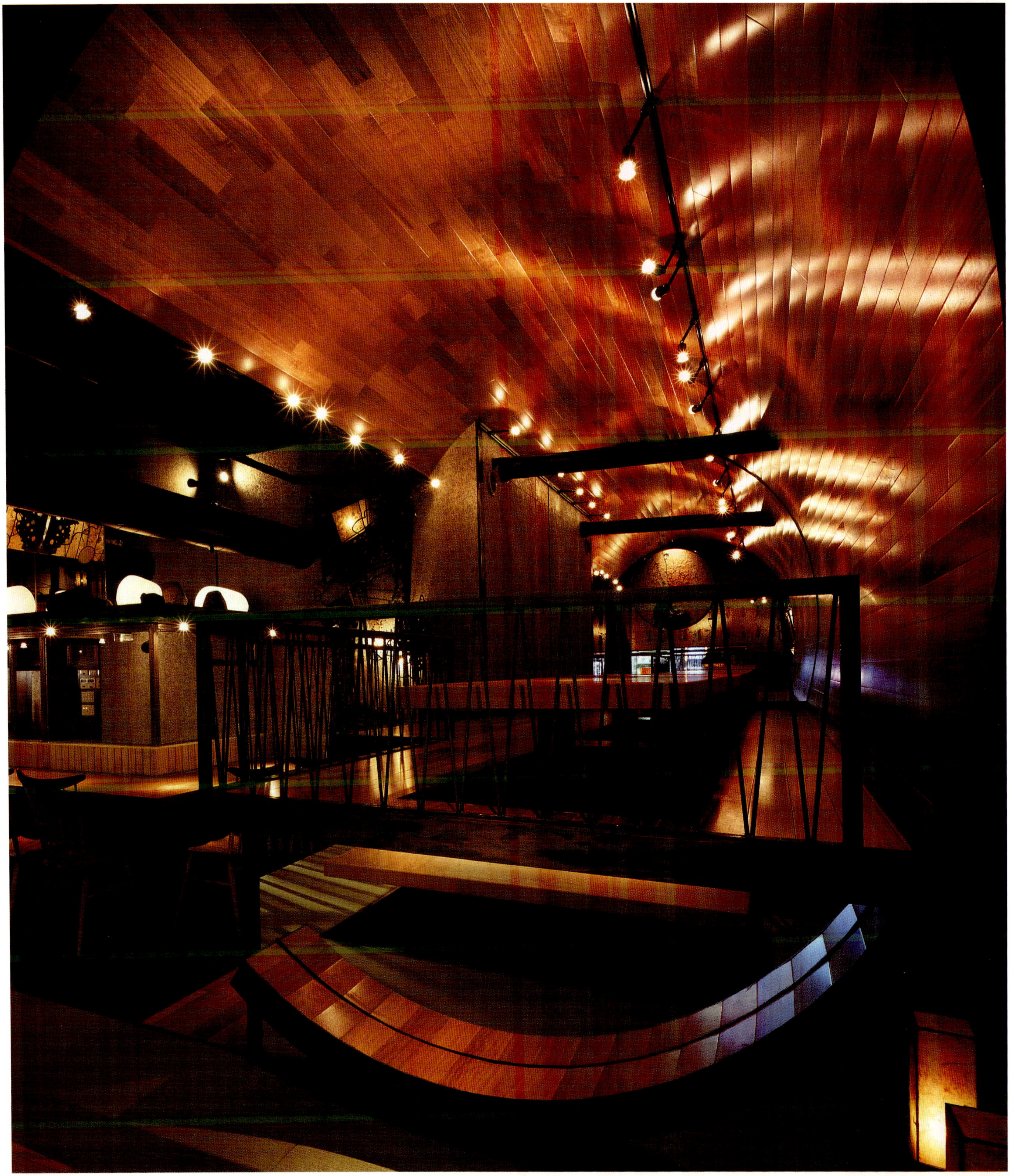

太田

白角屋

Shirokakuya

Exploring wooden worlds in the looking glass

To visually enlarge Shirokakuya's relatively small space, designer Yusaku Kaneshiro used the impact of the open arch in the wooden structure that seemed to wrap around the seats and tables and combined it with the optical elongation effect of mirrors. Mirrors were also used to enhance other spaces in this yakitori restaurant.

From the seating area on the second level, guests overlook the first level and enjoy the view of a Zen-influenced rock garden above the counter, where numerous black stones are intermittently juxtaposed with white glowing ones.

Tasteful lighting and the use of timber combine to create the interior's relaxing atmosphere. The illumination inside the arch enhances the natural colour of the wood. Here at the second level, guests can sit and place their legs in a square opening below the table. This is common in Japanese restaurants and makes it more comfortable for those who cannot sit directly on the floor for a long time. Other interior highlights include the modestly illuminated fantasy forms of the decoration, which complement the dark, unobtrusive Tatami-room styled walls.

真円と波が織りなす七色の表情を持つ空間。

PHOTOGRAPHY	Nacasa & Partners Inc.
DESIGNER	café co.
DESIGN TEAM	Yoshiyuki Morii
CONTRACTOR	Food Scope, Inc.
ADDRESS	Nishidobashi Bldg. 1~2 F, 8-3 Ginza, Chuo-ku, Tokyo 104-0061
PHONE	+81 (0) 3 3569 7733
AREA	600 m²
SEATING	150 seats, 11 private rooms
COMPLETED	2005

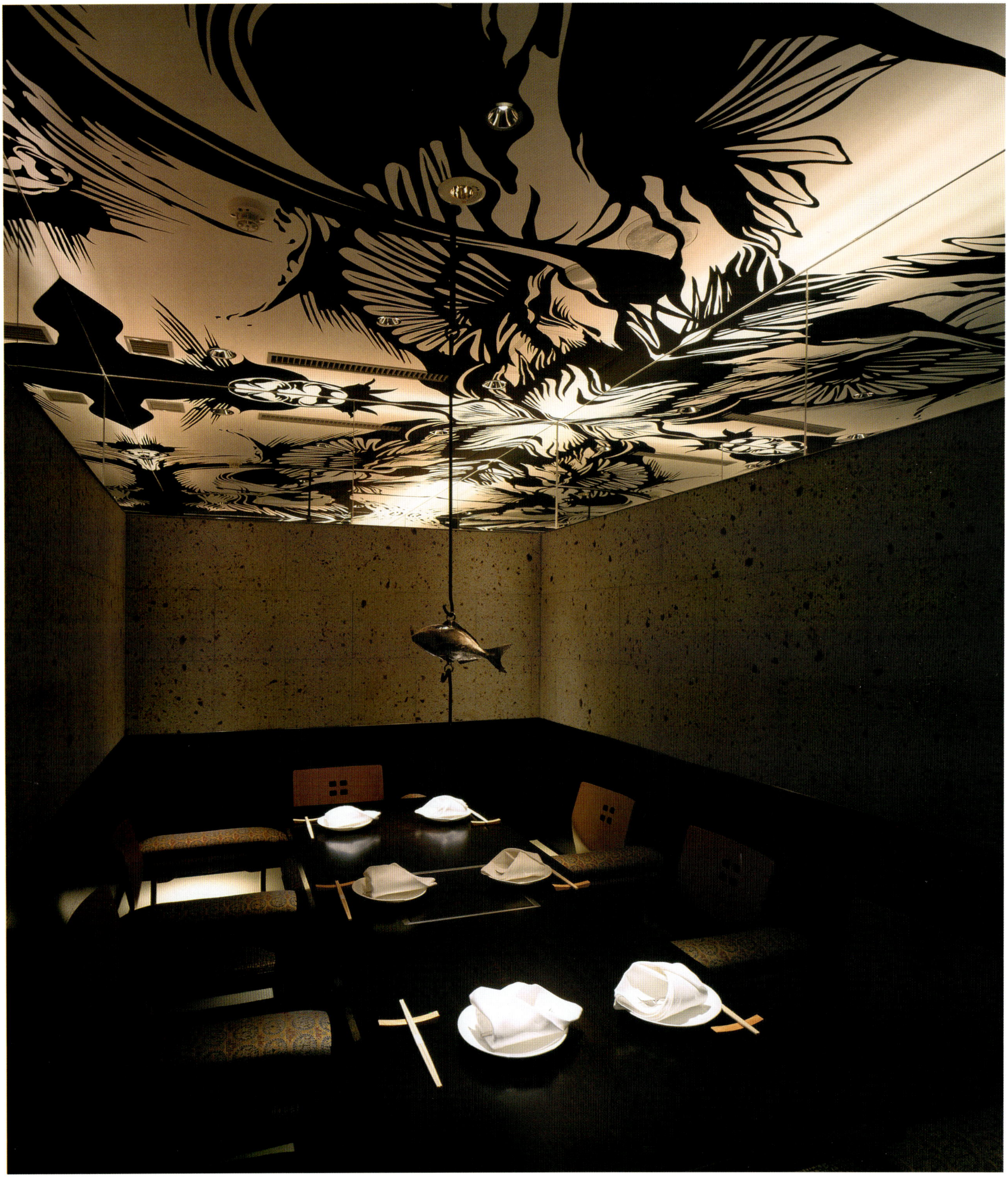

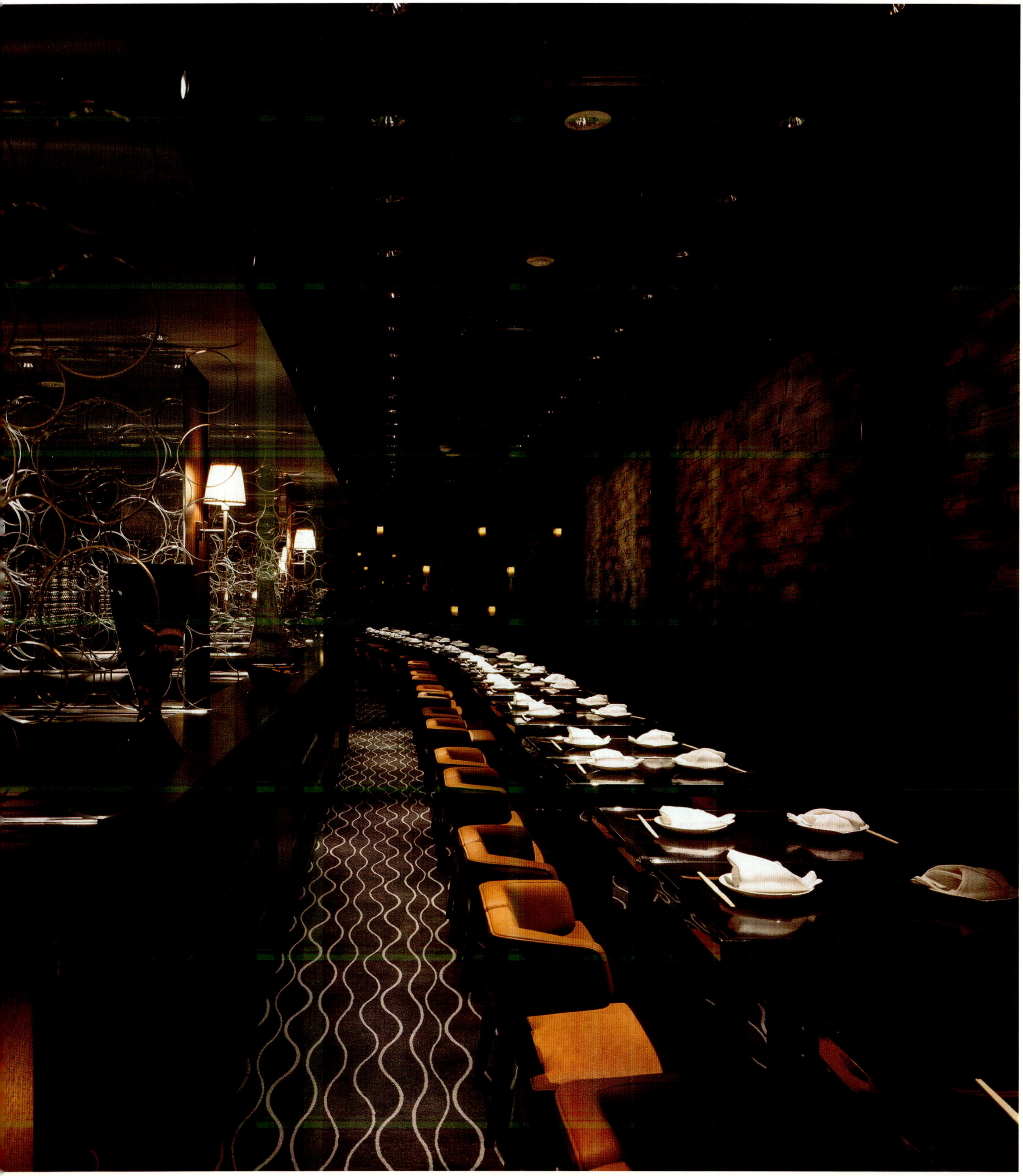

東京

マイモン

Maimon

Refreshingly cool blue

Oyster Bar & Charcoal Grill Maimon occupies two floors of a building in Ginza, close to Tokyo's most exclusive shopping area. Its location is convenient for shoppers as well as business people who frequent the area. The restaurant's elegant and stylish interior is clearly visible to passersby, which is necessary in order to stand out from the many other restaurants along this street. The cool neon blue illumination emanating from the façade, signboard, and the counter inside reflect the freshness that is requisite of an oyster bar.

On the first floor, the bar-counter sits in the centre, drawing the attention of guests. The cool blue illumination contrasts well with the dark and natural colours of the furniture, carpet and walls. A partition with circular motifs elegantly divides both sides of the counter as well as different seating areas. This circular motif can also be found on the second floor, where it is repeated as a pattern on the carpet and a decoration on the ceiling. On this level, the furnishings offer a cosy living room atmosphere with blue lighting on a huge bookshelf, comfortable armchairs and Japanese-style drawings of ostriches on a wall, adding a native touch to an otherwise western-style interior.

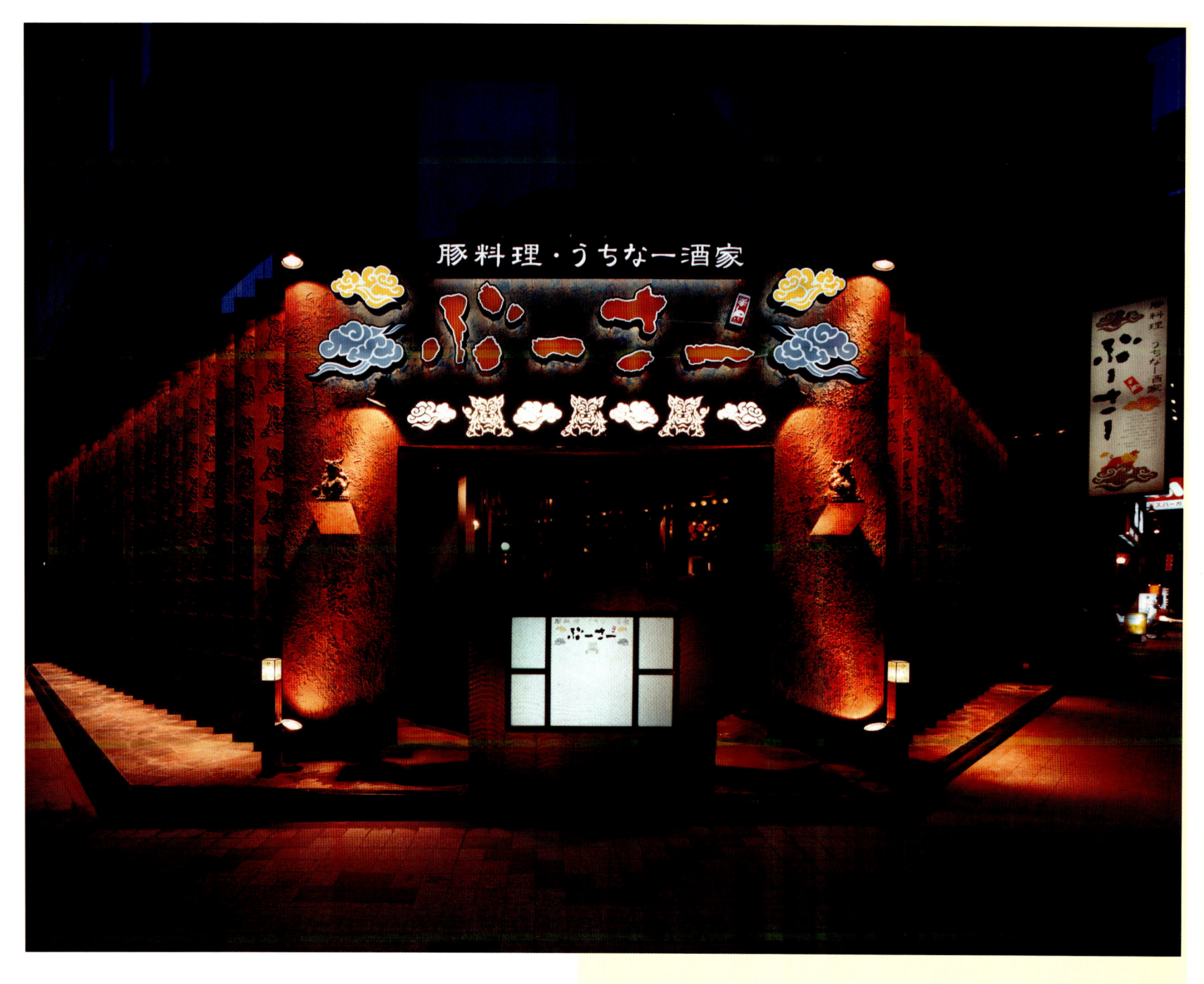

PHOTOGRAPHY	Masahiro Ishibashi
DESIGNER	Zoukei Syudan Co., Ltd.
DESIGN TEAM	Yusaku Kaneshiro, Hiromi Sato
CONTRACTOR	Gendai-Kikaku
ADDRESS	Okubo Bldg. 1F, Kasumi-cho, Yamagata City, Yamagata 990-0039
PHONE	+81 (0) 2 3633 9566
AREA	148 m²
SEATING	80 seats
COMPLETED	2004

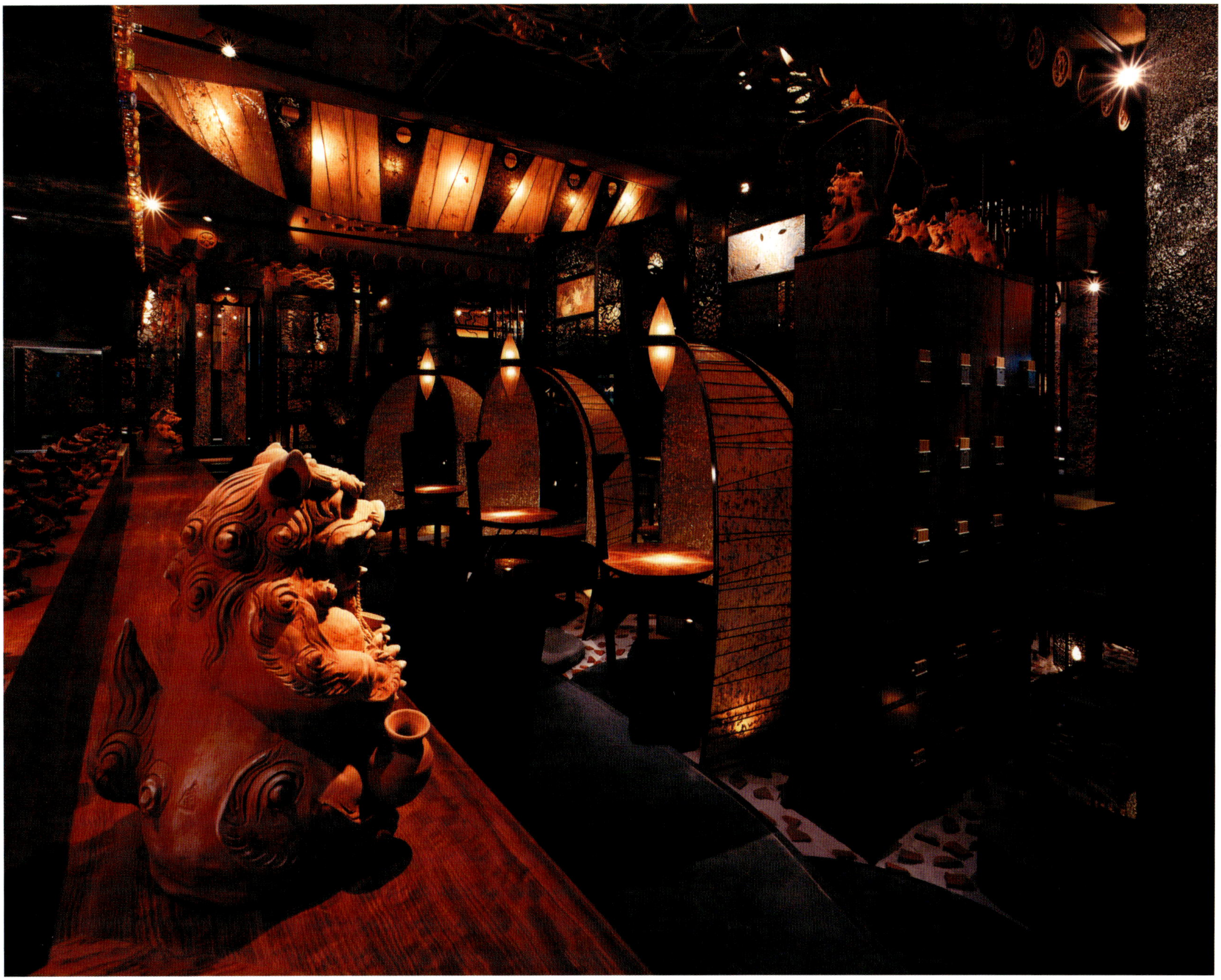

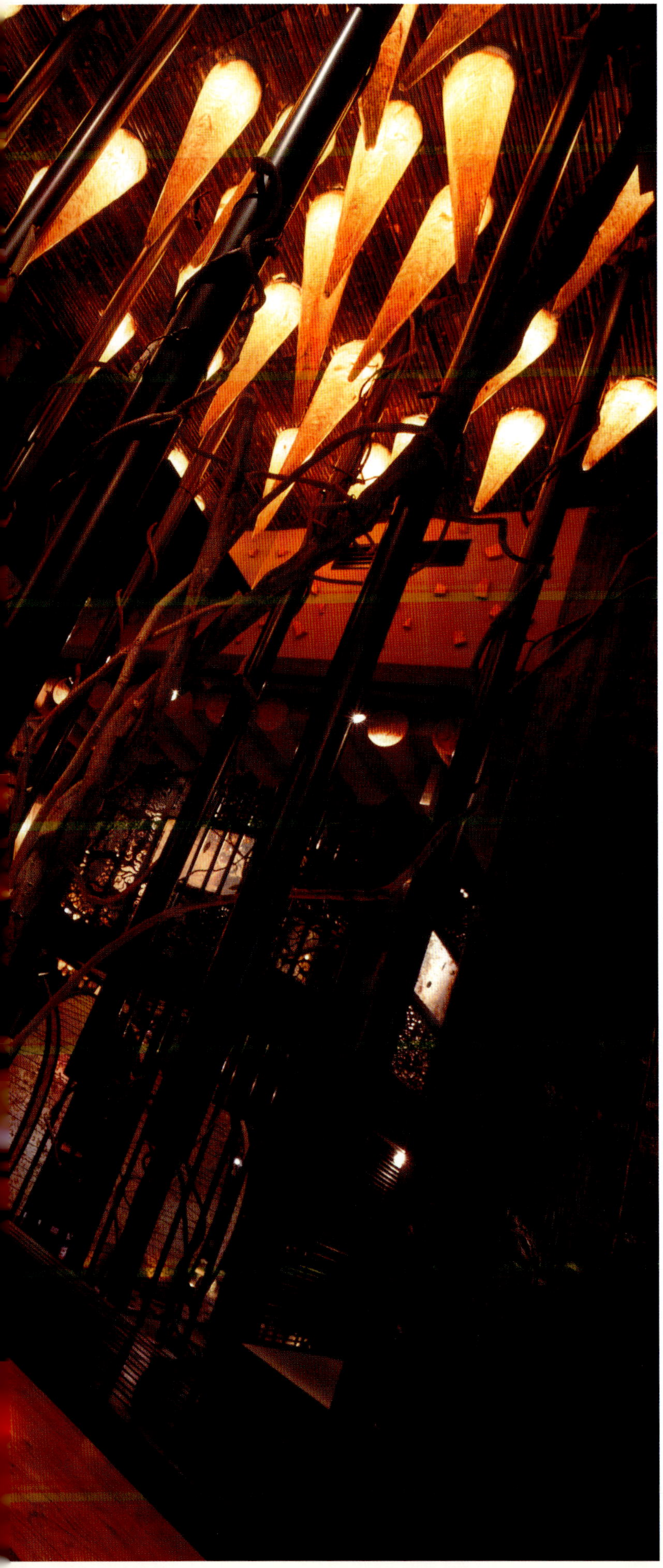
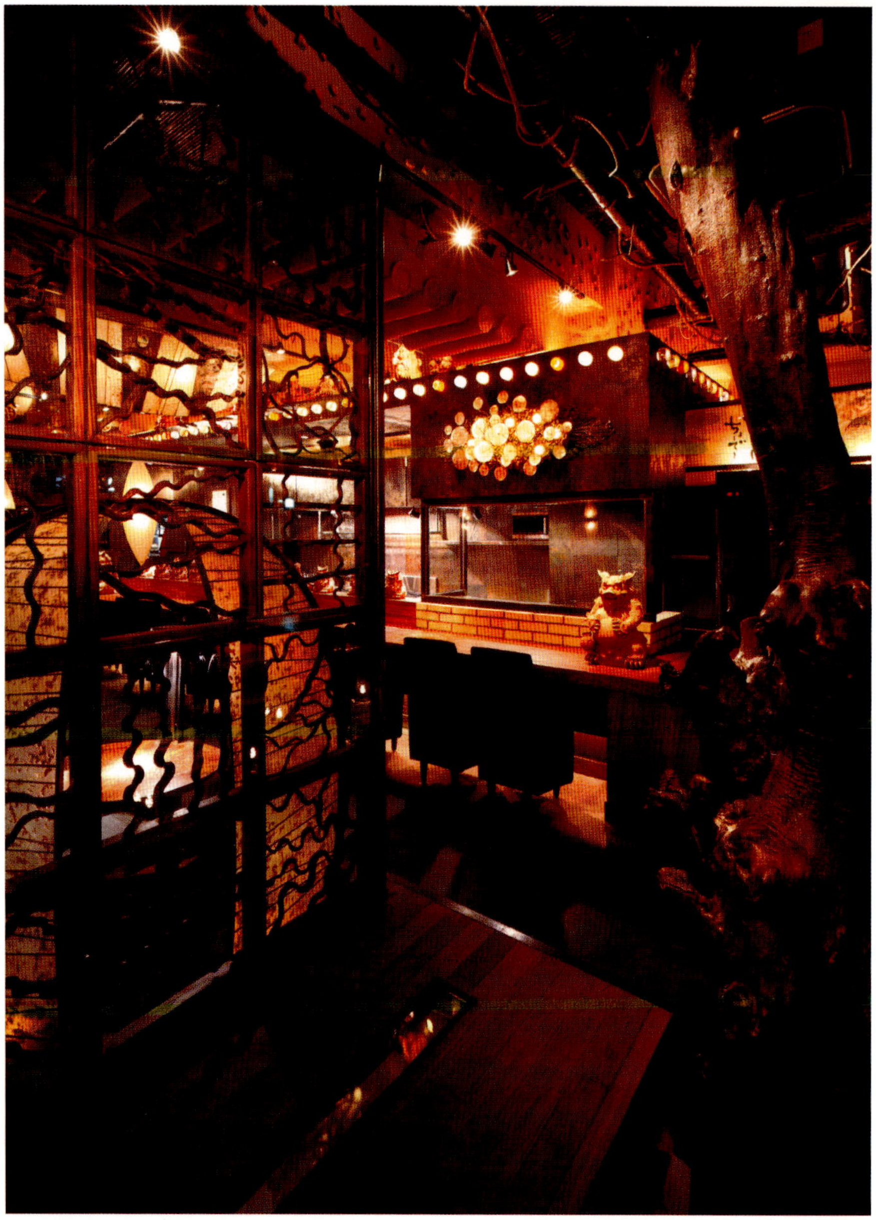
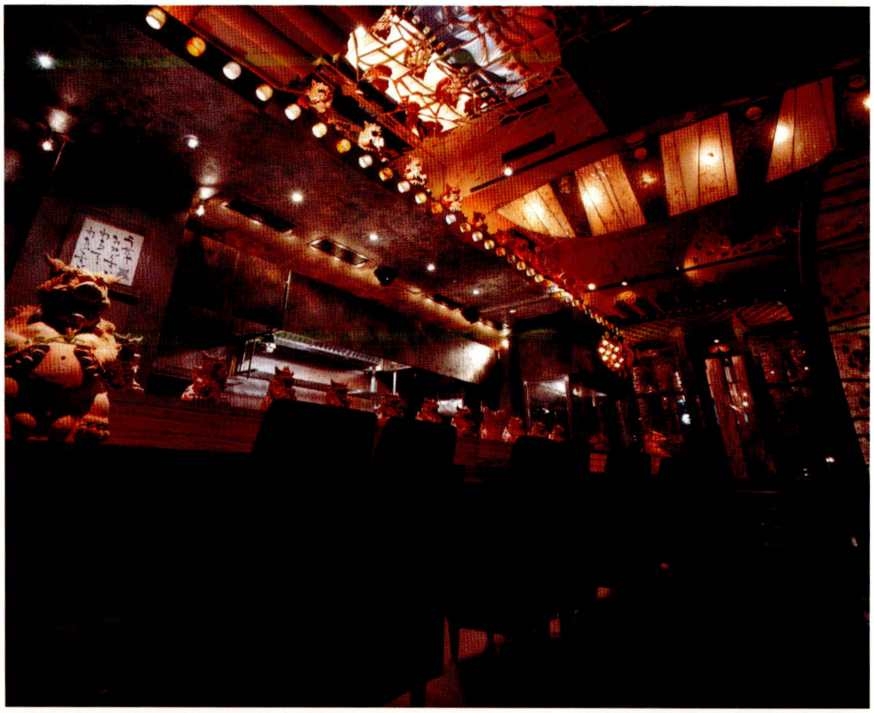

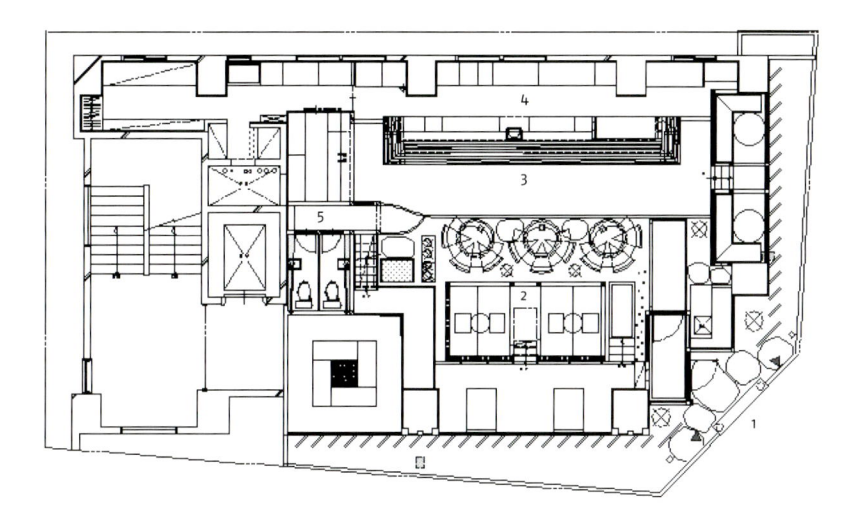

FIRST FLOOR
1 entrance
2 dining area
3 bar
4 kitchen
5 washroom

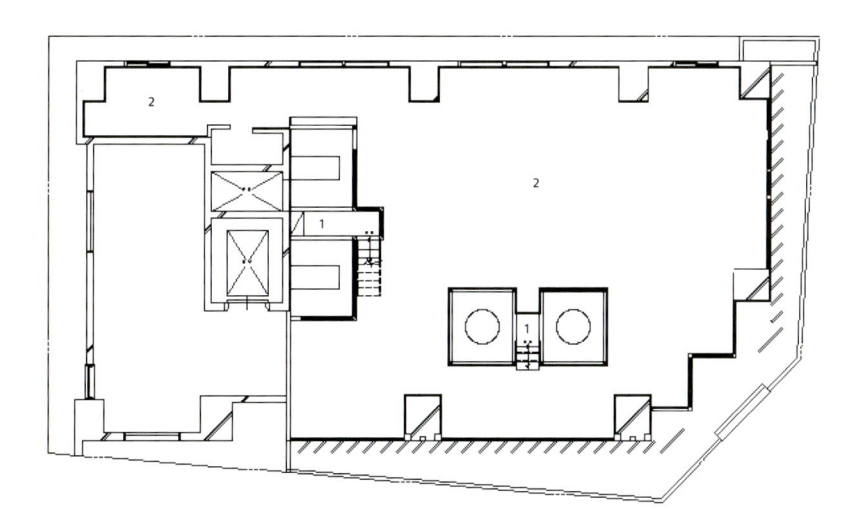

SECOND FLOOR
1 dining area
2 void

琉球の守護神が宿る、命ある曲線の世界。

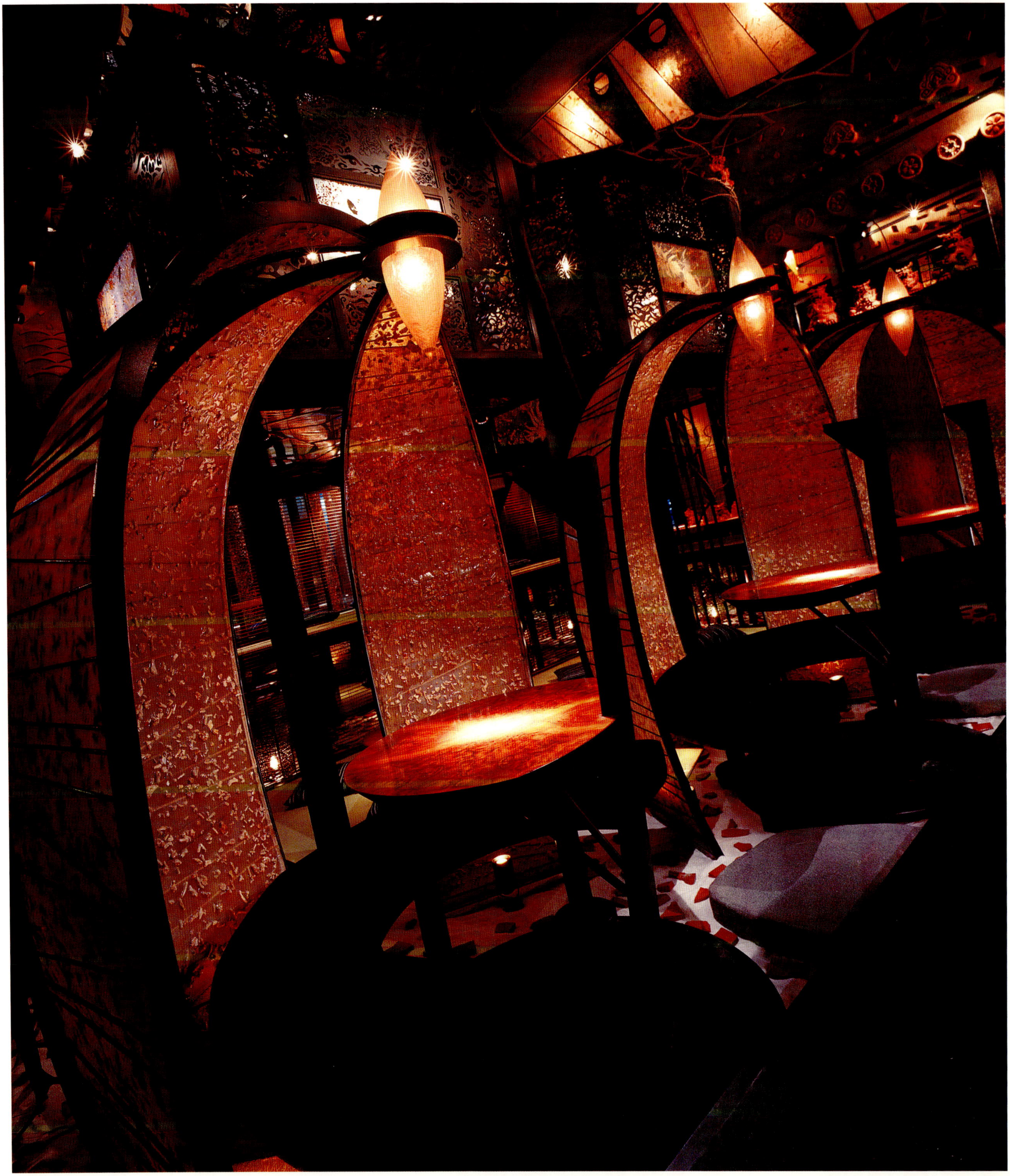

074　YAMAGATA

山形

ぶーさー

Bu'sa

Home of the spiritual gateway guardians

The Shisa is a special feature in Okinawa, Japan's southernmost prefecture. These cute looking lion-like creatures that are often placed in front of temples on the Ryukyu Islands are believed to serve as guardians that provide protection from evil spirits. Okinawans place them on their rooftops or in pairs flanking the entrance of their homes.

Tokyo-based designer Yusaku Kaneshiro who hails from Okinawa even integrates the funny lions into the restaurant design of Bu'sa in Yamagata Prefecture – bringing the warmth of Okinawan soil to the rather cold, mountainous north-western region of the Japanese main island. Shisa imprints bedeck the warmly coloured façade, while a pair at the doorway keeps malicious spirits away.

The place's exterior is so welcoming that even vegetarians find it hard to ignore, despite the fact that the main dish of the restaurant is pork – a common ingredient in Okinawan kitchens. The name Bu'sa combines the Japanese characters for "Shisa" and "buta" (pork).

Inside, the lion figures adorn the whole place; some hold their little round bellies like customers who have eaten too much, others sit looking tipsy with a little goblet in one paw. There is even a Shisa holding a surfboard amidst the decoration. According to Kaneshiro, they were all specially handcrafted in Okinawa for the purpose of enriching the restaurant's interior. Even the raw materials –such as glass, tiles and coral parts that are used for decoration– were transported from Okinawa to create this unique atmosphere.

As with many Japanese restaurants, guests must leave their shoes behind before entering a designated dining area – typically rooms with Tatami mats. These are then put into special shoe lockers, to which diners keep the respective wooden square keys until they leave the restaurant.

PHOTOGRAPHY	Masahiro Ishibashi
DESIGNER	Zoukei Syudan Co.,Ltd.
DESIGN TEAM	Yusaku Kaneshiro, Miho Umeda
CONTRACTOR	Gendai-Kikaku
ADDRESS	1-69 Konida, Yamagata City, Yamagata 990-0035
PHONE	+81 (0) 2 3615 7166
AREA	661 m²
SEATING	202 seats
COMPLETED	2004

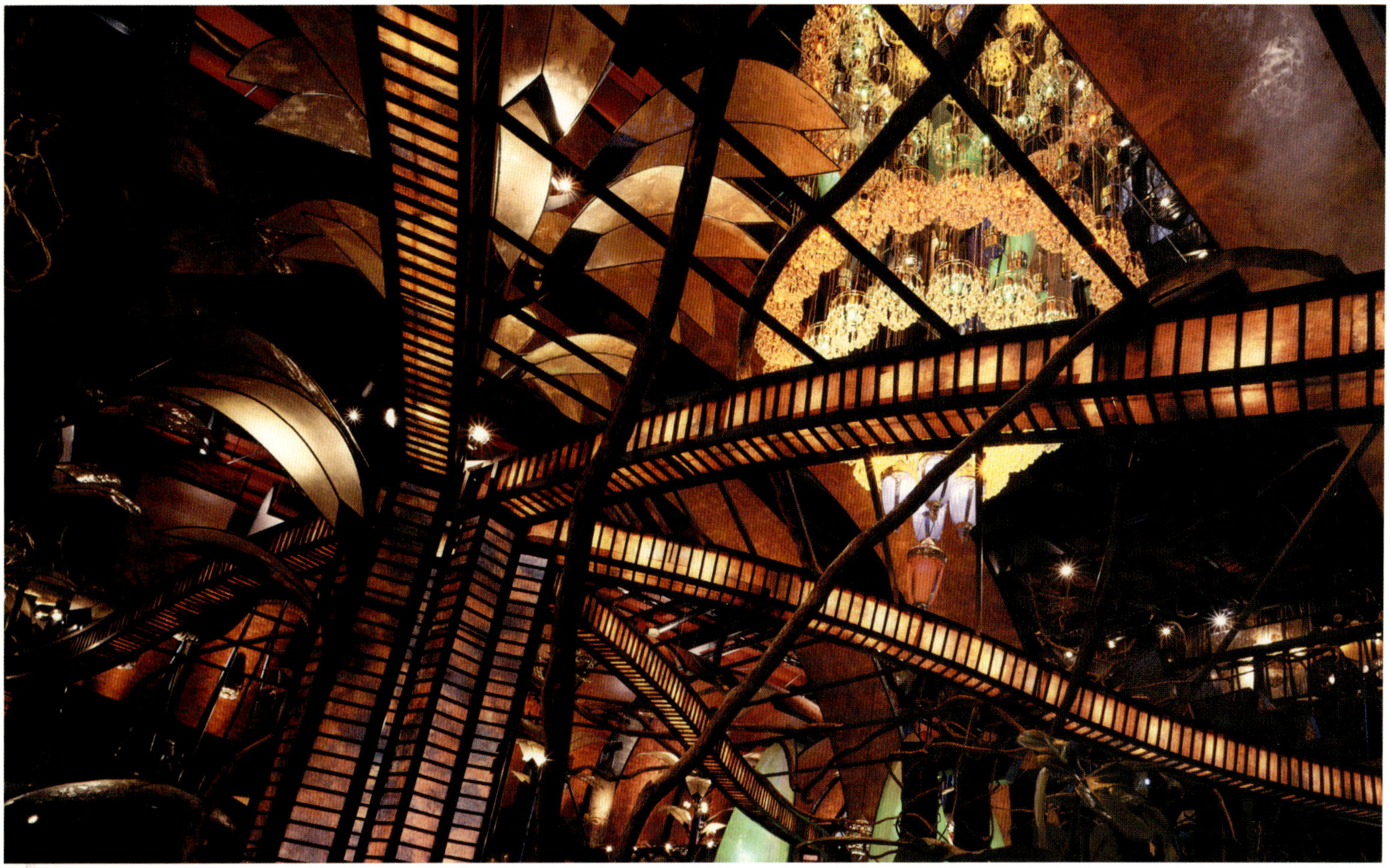
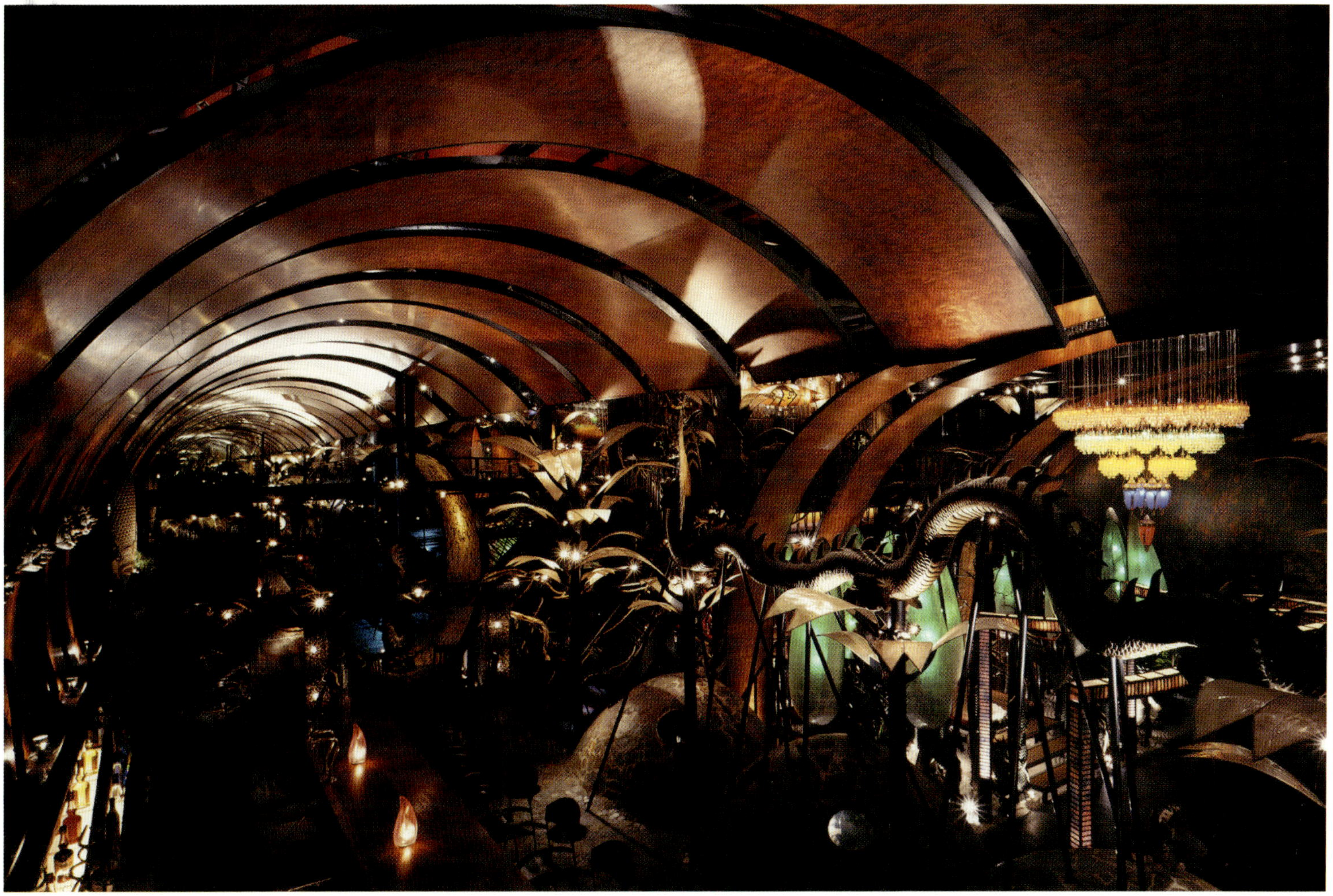

FIRST FLOOR

1 entrance
2 cashier
3 dining area
4 bar
5 kitchen
6 staff room
7 stock room
8 washroom

SECOND FLOOR

1 bedseat

FIRST FLOOR

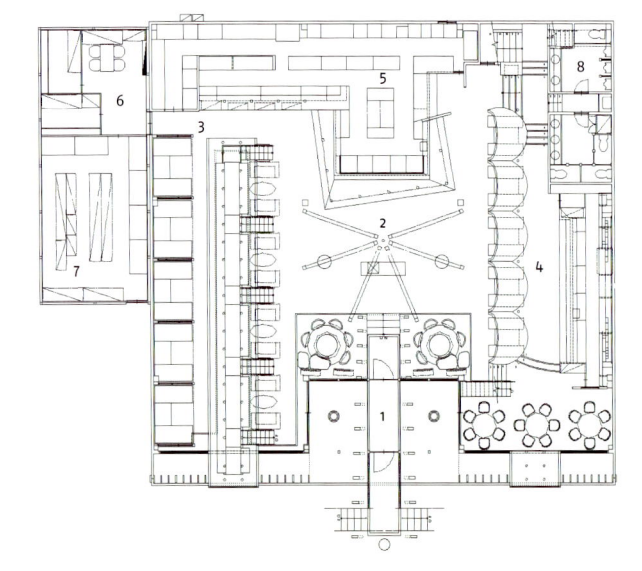

SECOND FLOOR

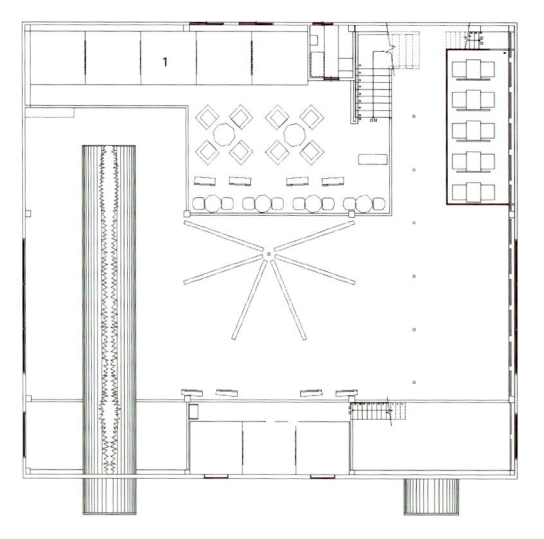

幻想の神が舞い降りる、妖しく心躍る時空。

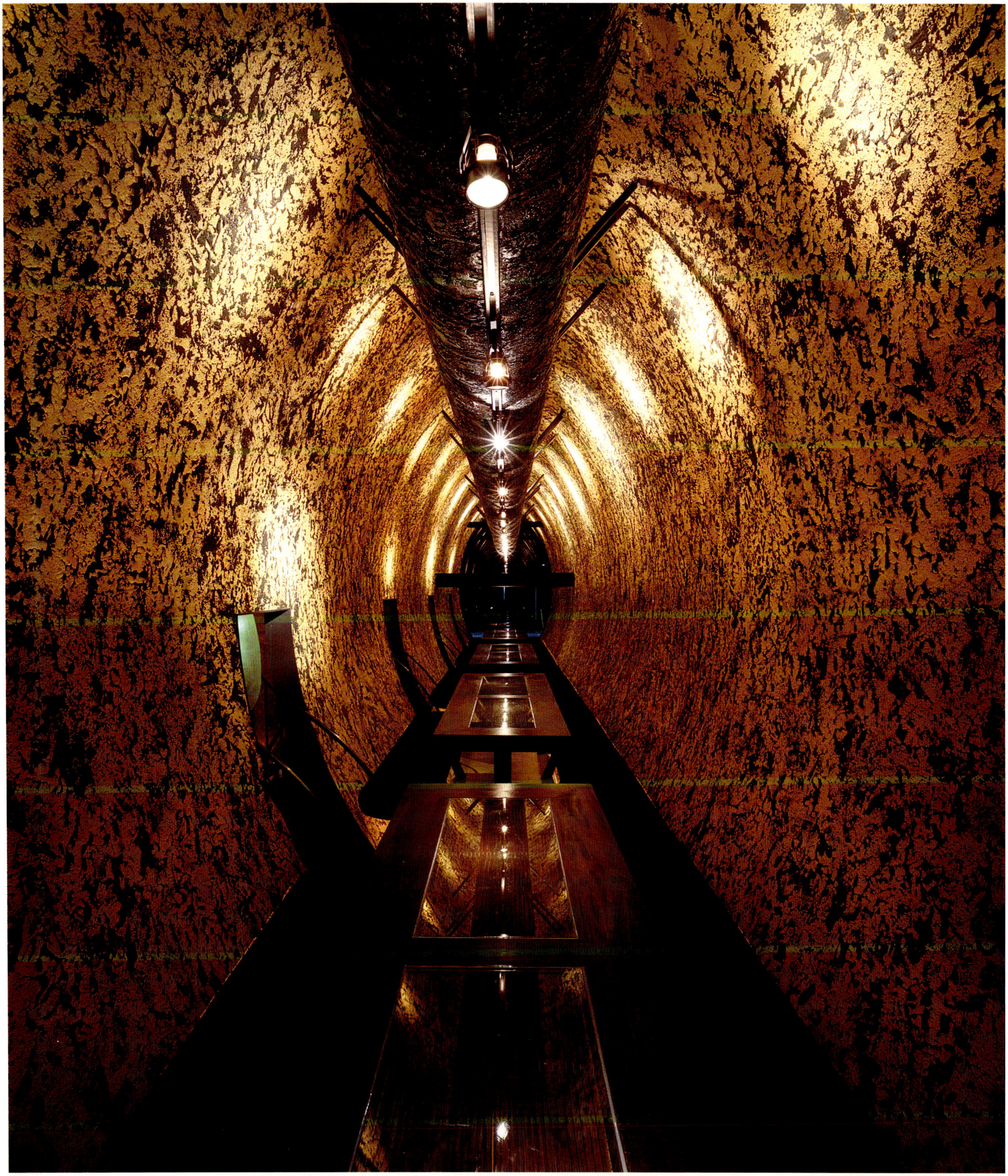

山形

タイタイ

Thai Thai Yamagata
A truly divine experience

The building that houses Thai Thai is huge and so is its interior space. Designer Yusaku Kaneshiro and his team had 661 sqm of space to let their imaginations run free. The awesome result leaves its visitors at a loss for words.

The motifs on display include about 50 Asian deities including Ganesha and Buddha, as well as dragon sculptures, the most spectacular of which is a long flying dragon on metal bars measuring more than twenty metres long.

A great 30-metre long tunnel extends through the whole building, giving one the impression of being in a cave upon entering via a flight of stairs. The tunnel extends partially through the facade of the building so that visitors can preview the exceptional design that awaits them inside.

Small cocoon-shaped caves serve as private dining hideaways. The warm colour of the furniture and the marbled earthen walls of the interior create a comfortable, naturally relaxing atmosphere. Atop all this sits the restaurant's bar, a sign of Kaneshiro's preference for integrating different levels into an interior. He understands that while such structures do make it tough for the service personnel, the most important thing is that guests enjoy their time fully. With many differently designed areas in the interior, guests can explore new spaces every time they visit this restaurant.

PHOTOGRAPHY	Masaya Yoshimura
DESIGNER	Fantastic Design Works
DESIGN TEAM	Katsunori Suzuki (sketch for wall design by Kelly Chen)
CONTRACTOR	TRY Inc. / avex Planning & Development Inc.
ADDRESS	B1F, Lexington Aoyama, 5-11-9, Minami-Aoyama, Minato-ku, Tokyo 107-0062
PHONE	+81 (0) 3 5469 7700
AREA	475 m²
SEATING	196 seats
COMPLETED	2006

妖しさという美意識が、人を魅了してやまない。

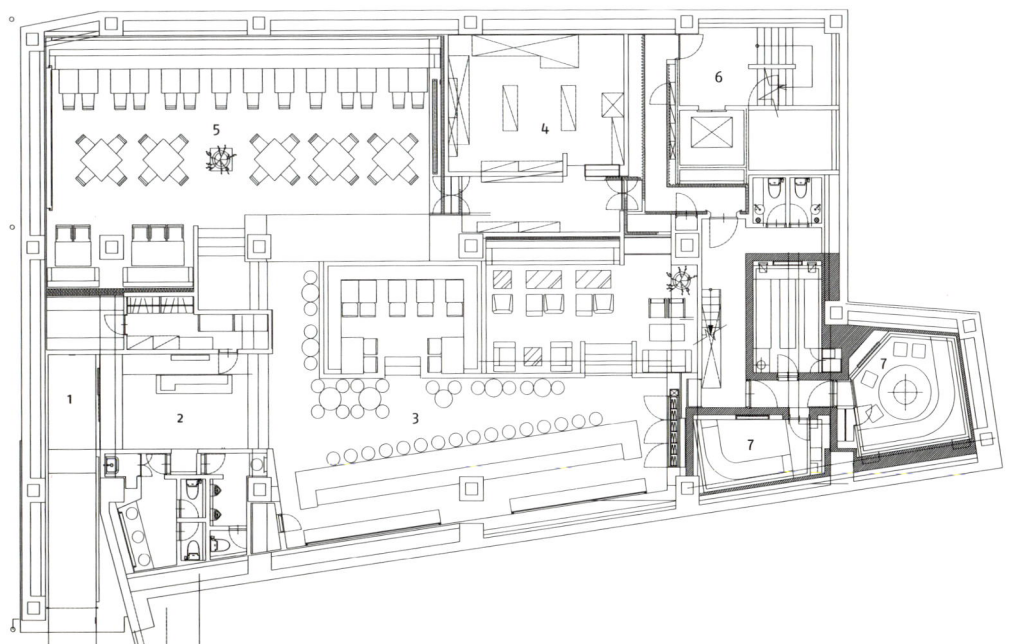

FLOORPLAN

1. entrance
2. cashier
3. bar
4. kitchen
5. dining area
6. VIP entrance
7. karaoke

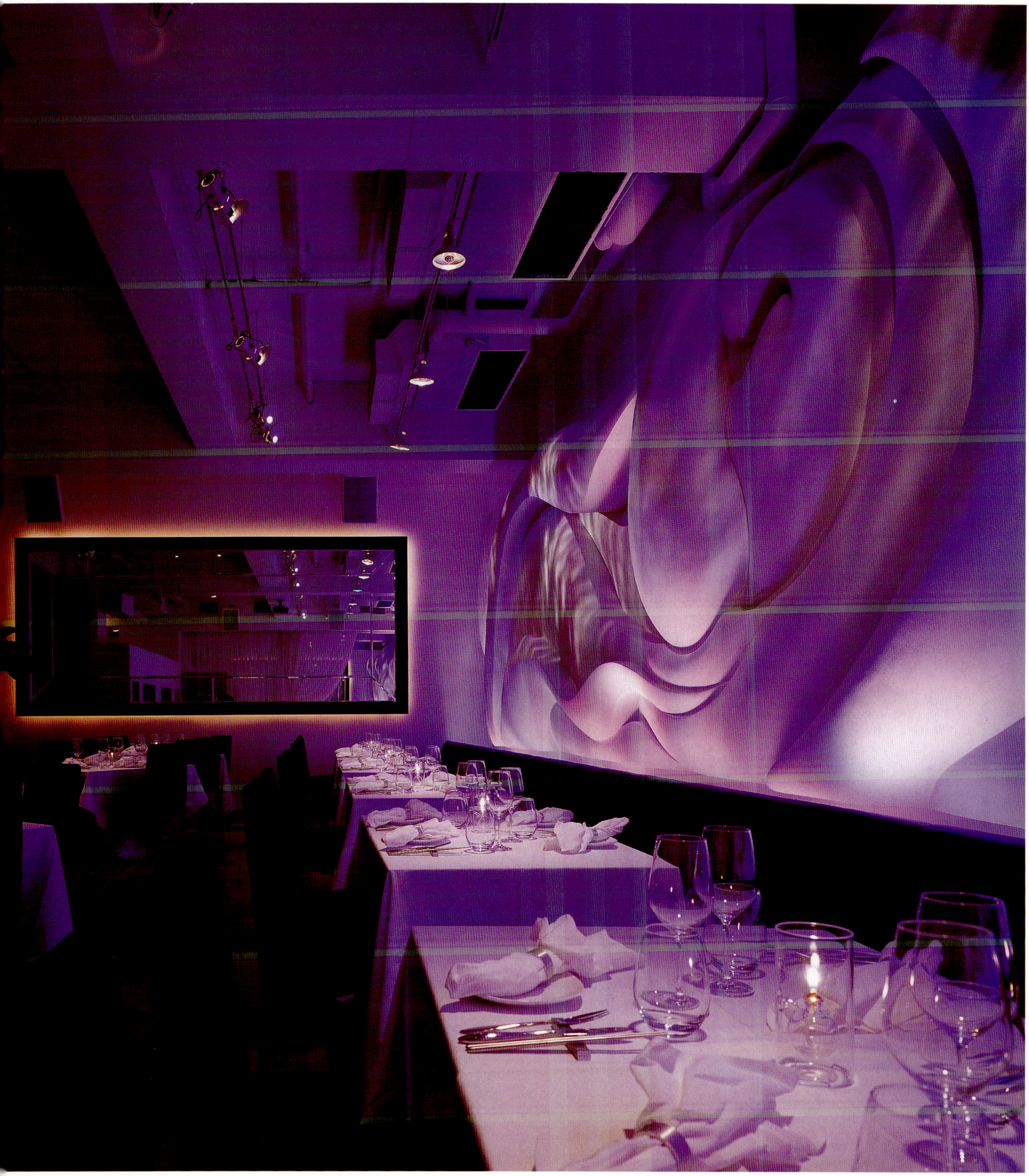

東京

アリュックス

Alux

A lavish presentation from kitchen to hall

avex, one of the world's largest independent record labels and probably the largest in Japan, opened this restaurant in Aoyama, one of Tokyo's hippest neighbourhoods. Driven by the motto of "all luxury", it was named Alux and lived up to its name, starting with the idea of getting a star to design the wall of the main dining area. Hong Kong-based actress and singer Kelly Chen, who studied Graphic Design at the Parsons School of Design in New York City, was chosen for the task. She sketched the terrific shape which the wall of the main dining area would take. Enhanced with beautiful illumination, it became the focal point of the space. Designer Katsunori Suzuki, renowned for the design of J-Pop Café in Tokyo and later Taipei, was responsible for the implementation of the wall's design and the other features of this unique establishment.

Alux lavished special attention not just on its interior but on its staff as well. All the waiters, waitresses and kitchen staff wear uniforms specially designed under the "Emporio Armani" label, while music is played in the kitchen to make the workplace more fun. With all the right rhythms in place, the chefs can be inspired to add new dishes to the "Novelle Cucina Italo Giapponese" menu, a fusion of Italian and Japanese delicacies.

伝統と象徴、そして存在感が調和する亜空間。

PHOTOGRAPHY	Masaya Yoshimura (Nacasa & Partners Inc.)
DESIGNER	Fantastic Design Works
DESIGN TEAM	Katsunori Suzuki
CONTRACTOR	Diamond Dining
ADDRESS	Kinsia Bldg. 5F, Kodobashi, Sumida-ku, Tokyo 103-0022
PHONE	+81 (0) 3 5624 0320
AREA	176 m²
SEATING	105 seats
COMPLETED	2006

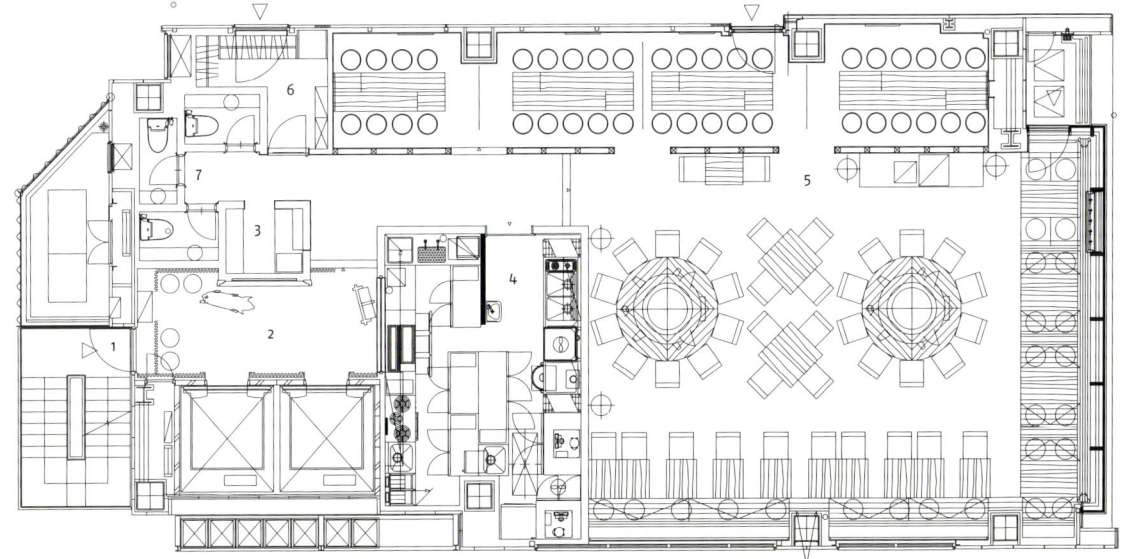

FLOORPLAN

1   entrance
2   reception
3   cashier
4   kitchen
5   dining area
6   staff room
7   washroom

本日の特選豚
葉さわやかポーク
ビタミンEが通常の豚肉の3倍!
オレイン酸は8〜12%アップ!
〜さわやかバラ肉のダッチオーブン〜
¥1580

東京

ベルサイユの豚

Le Porc de Versailles

Garden parties in piggy playland

The theme of this restaurant is based on a fictional account of Marie Antoinette. Since designer Katsunori Suzuki is a big fan of Japanese manga, he adapted "The Rose of Versailles," a love story about the former Queen of France, for the restaurant's name "Le Porc de Versailles".

The restaurant's design reflects the story of Marie Antoinette who purportedly loved pigs and had a barn for them in one of the Versailles palace gardens. According to the story, a special kind of pig called "Celebrity Pork" was reared and commemorative marble pig statues remain there until today. The main dining area therefore re-creates the image of that porcine garden, with huge pig statues that turn 360 degrees in one hour throughout its interior. The main dish is pork, and guests can select pork delicacies from all over the world.

At the entrance area, a huge oil painting of Marie Antoinette welcomes the guests. Drawn by Takeshi Yoshida, Suzuki's artist friend, the oil painting is based on an original that depicts Marie Antoinette cradling a child. In Yoshida's version, Marie carries a funny-looking little pig on her lap instead. The painting took Yoshida one month to complete.

Furthermore, one of the walls is decorated with a curtain of white and black ping pong balls that form the word "Versailles". Ping pong balls are used because they are light and inexpensive. In an adjoining room, chalk boards with pig drawings are used as menu displays or for joke-telling sessions during parties.

FLOORPLAN

1. entrance
2. dining area
3. bar
4. kitchen
5. washroom

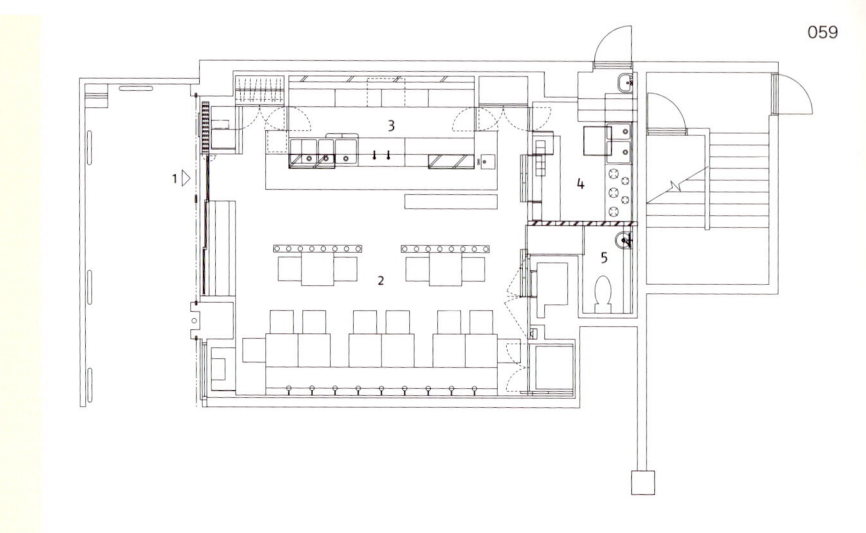

PHOTOGRAPHY	Shinichi Sato (Sato Shinichi Photo Studio)
DESIGNER	Love the Life
DESIGN TEAM	Akemi Katsuno & Takashi Yagi
	[Graphic designer : Yuji Oshimoto (Samohung)]
CONTRACTOR	Atsushi & Eri Ikeda
ADDRESS	2-17-12, Utsukushigaoka, Aoba-ku,
	Yokohama City, Kanagawa 225-0002
PHONE	+81 (0) 4 5903 5010
AREA	65 m²
SEATING	19 seats (+6 standing)
COMPLETED	2004

すべてを削ぎ落とし味を追求する表舞台。

赤ワイン		白ワイン	
・COSAN TINTO		・EL COTO BLANCO	
コサン ティント	¥2200	エルコト ブランコ	¥2300
・VEGA ESTEBAN TINTO		・VEGA ESTEBAN BLANCO	
ベガ エスデバン ティント	¥2500	ベガ エスデバン ブランコ	¥2500
・SIGLO XVI		・CONDES DE ALBAREI	
シグロ 16	¥2700	コンデス デ アルバレイ	¥3800
・EL COTO CRIANZA		CAVA (スパークリングワイン)	
エル コト クリアンサ	¥3050		
・MONTE TORO CRIANZA		・RONDEL	
モンテ トロ クリアンサ	¥4400	ロンデル	¥2800
・RAMON BILBAO		・MONTSARRA	
ラモン ビルバオ	¥4600	モンサラ	¥3600
・VINA MAYOR TINTO ROBLE			
ビニャ マヨール ティント ロブレ	¥5200		
・VINA MAYOR CRIANZA			
ビニャ マヨール クリアンサ	¥5800		

横浜

シンパティカ

Simpatica
Of black olives and pins

Featuring an illuminated wall decorated with tubes and little orbs of light hanging at the end of long, thin tubes from the ceiling, Simpatica's design is simple yet striking. The bar and tapas restaurant – a rare treat in Japan - is located in Utsukushigaoka, a residential area of Yokohama that is only about 40 years old and still growing. Many high-rise apartments are being built here to accommodate the young families who cannot afford Tokyo's exorbitant rents.

Coming home after a long working day, Utsukushigaoka's residents are invited to unwind at Simpatica. Located next to the main street, Simpatica's welcoming atmosphere is openly visible through the huge window at the entrance.

The interior's main motif is derived from the image of a black olive with a pin stuck in it. The colour of the interior is primarily dark purple - the real colour of the black olive - and silver. The olive design can even be found on the umbrella stand at the entrance and on the chairs.

PHOTOGRAPHY	Ellen Nepilly
DESIGNER	Hideo Horikawa Architect & Associates
DESIGN TEAM	Hideo Horikawa
CONTRACTOR	Akira Kasuya
ADDRESS	Hayashi Bldg. 4F, 1-14-7 Kabukicho, Shinjuku-ku, Tokyo 160-0021
PHONE	+81 (0) 3 3202 3061
AREA	250 m²
SEATING	200 seats, 6 private rooms
COMPLETED	2004

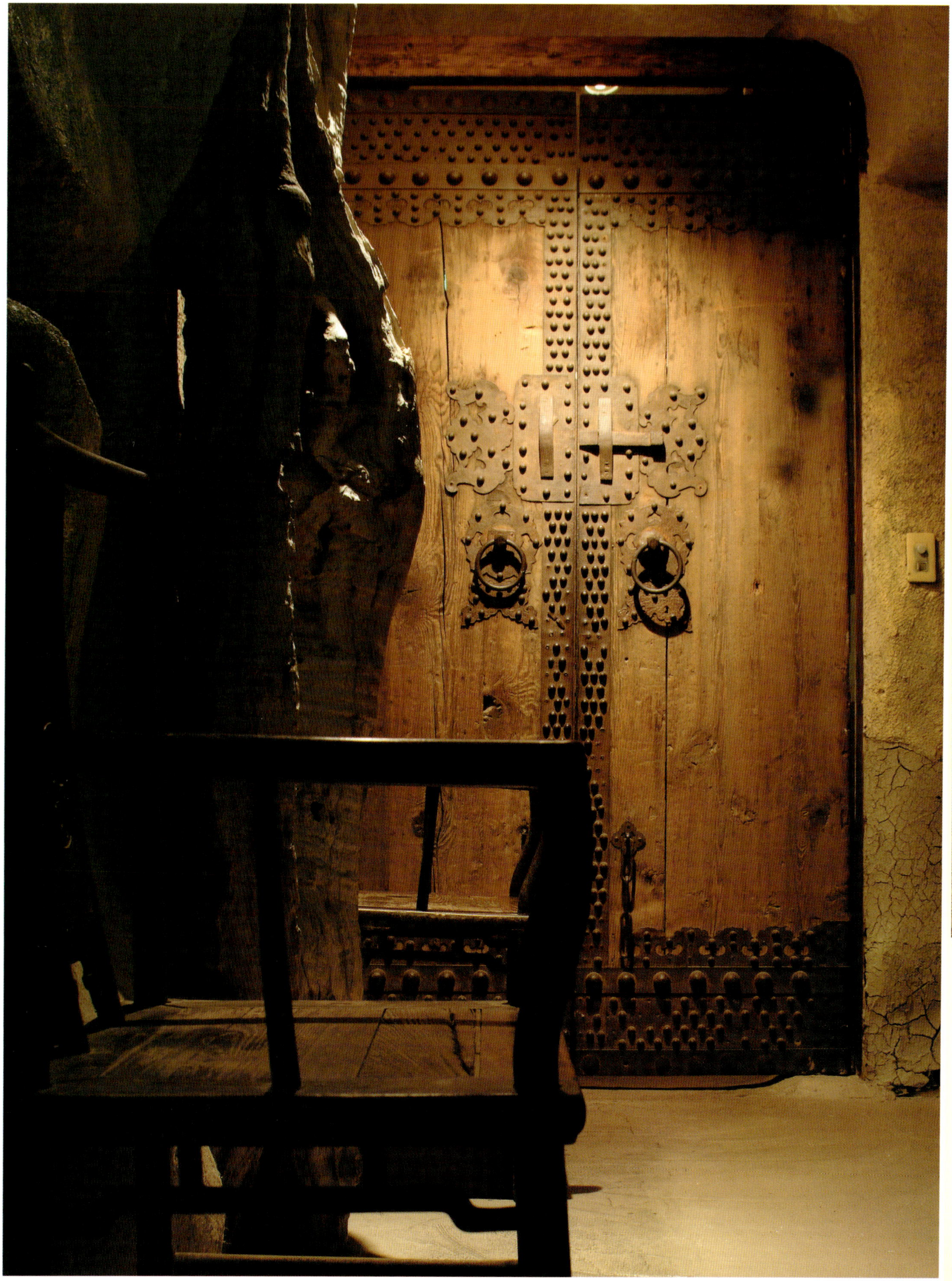

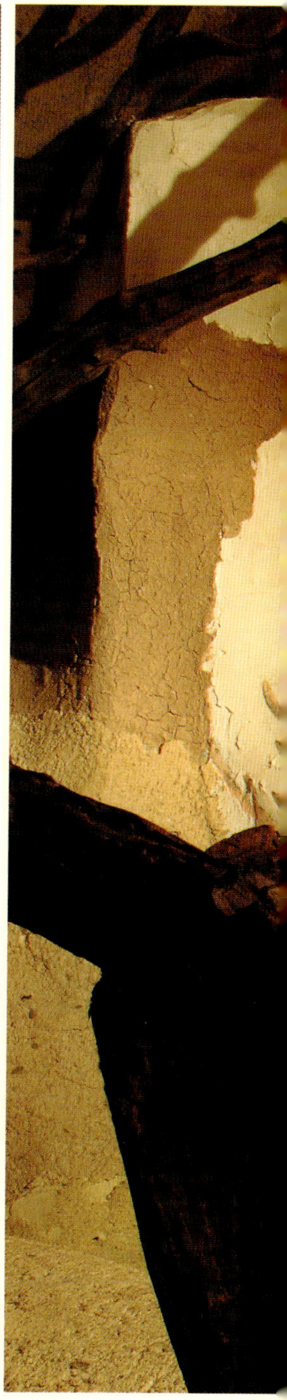

FLOORPLAN

1 entrance
2 dining area
3 kitchen
4 karaoke area
5 washroom

大地に抱かれ護られるような、やすらぎ深き空間。

鳴砂山

東京

異邦人

The Stranger

Bringing the beauty of the desert to town

The client asked architect Hideo Horikawa to design the interior for "The Stranger" in Tokyo's famous Kabukicho, an entertainment district that offers everything from high class restaurants to love hotels and hostess clubs. People who visit the "town that never sleeps" mostly go there for one purpose – fun partying. The Stranger's interior therefore had to have space for partying while offering guests a welcoming and comfortable atmosphere. The main task was to create an interior that didn't make guests feel like they were in a restaurant.

With a menu consisting of Chinese cuisine, Horikawa determined that the theme for The Stranger should be based on ancient China. He was struck by the notion of the ancient Chinese Silk Road and Taklamakan, China's biggest desert, and decided to draw ideas from that environment. The Stranger's big party room and six private rooms combined to create the concept of a desert inside a building.

Inside the private rooms, guests can sit on the floor amidst cushions, or climb up to the integrated lofts, where they can sing karaoke, watch films and TV, or just sit and chat. Shoes must be placed outside the rooms, and if guests need to use the restroom, slippers are conveniently placed before each door for their use. The doors to each room can be closed so that each party can enjoy privacy without disturbing others with their singing.

The biggest room is designed for big company parties and offers space for up to 100 guests. The tree trunk in the middle of the room, together with another at the entrance, was specially imported from Burma where they had been preserved in a lake for over 400 years. The entrance door is an antique piece from China. To give the interior the look of real earth, the walls were plastered with differently coloured layers of stucco. For a final artistic flourish to the interior, Horikawa asked two artists for their input. Yuko Kobayakawa drew the image of a Chinese woman and wrote a Chinese poem, while Leonardo Kii drew a Mandala on the walls of specific rooms.

PHOTOGRAPHY	Nacasa & Partners Inc.
DESIGNER	Nomura Co., Ltd.
DESIGN TEAM	Ryu Kosaka, Toshiyuki Taya / A.N.D.
CONTRACTOR	Ramla
ADDRESS	Ebisu Garden Place Glass Square, 4-20-4, Ebisu, Shibuya-ku, Tokyo 150-6090
PHONE	+81 (0) 3 5791 7666
AREA	850 m²
SEATING	360 seats
COMPLETED	2003

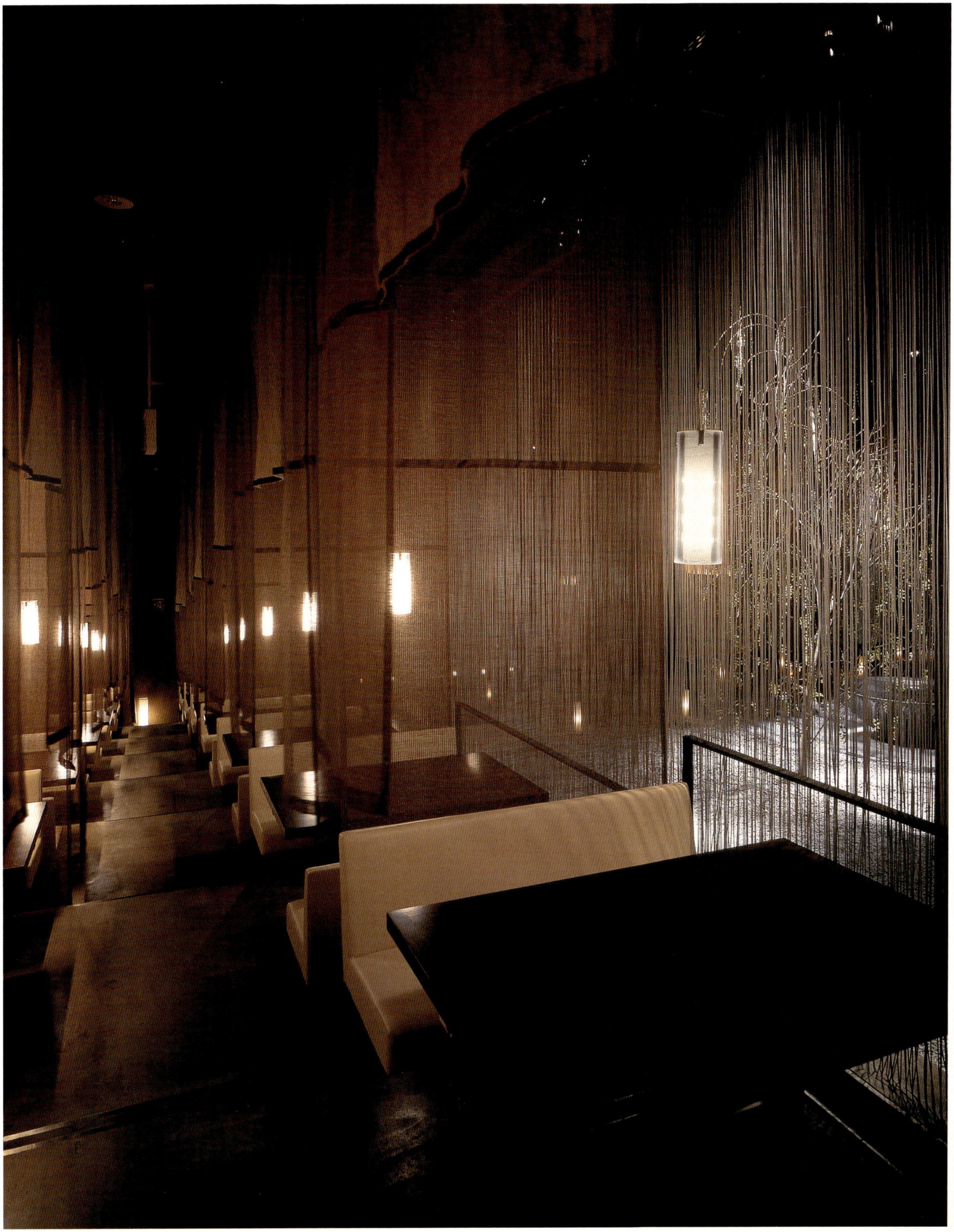

FIRST FLOOR

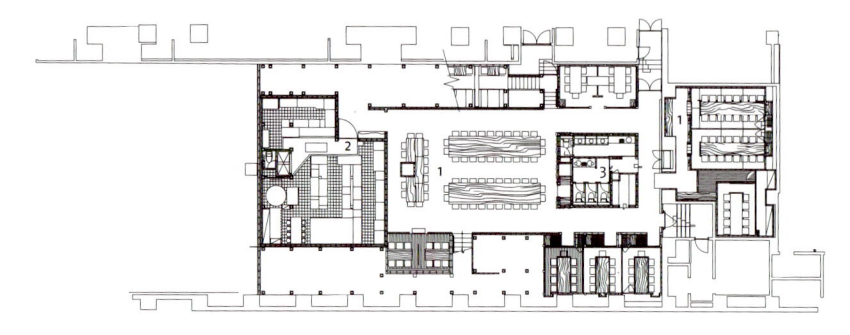

047

SECOND FLOOR

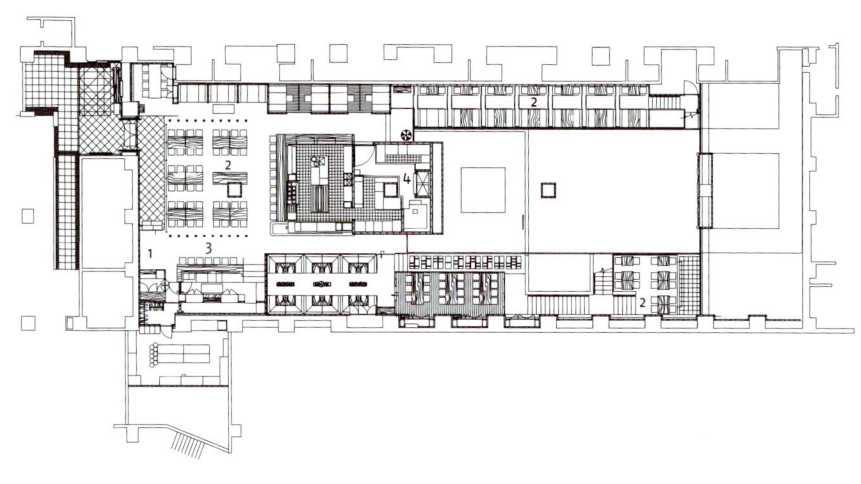

FIRST FLOOR
1   dining area
2   kitchen
3   washroom

SECOND FLOOR
1   entrance
2   dining area
3   bar
4   kitchen

まるで優しい雨に抱かれるような時のしじま。

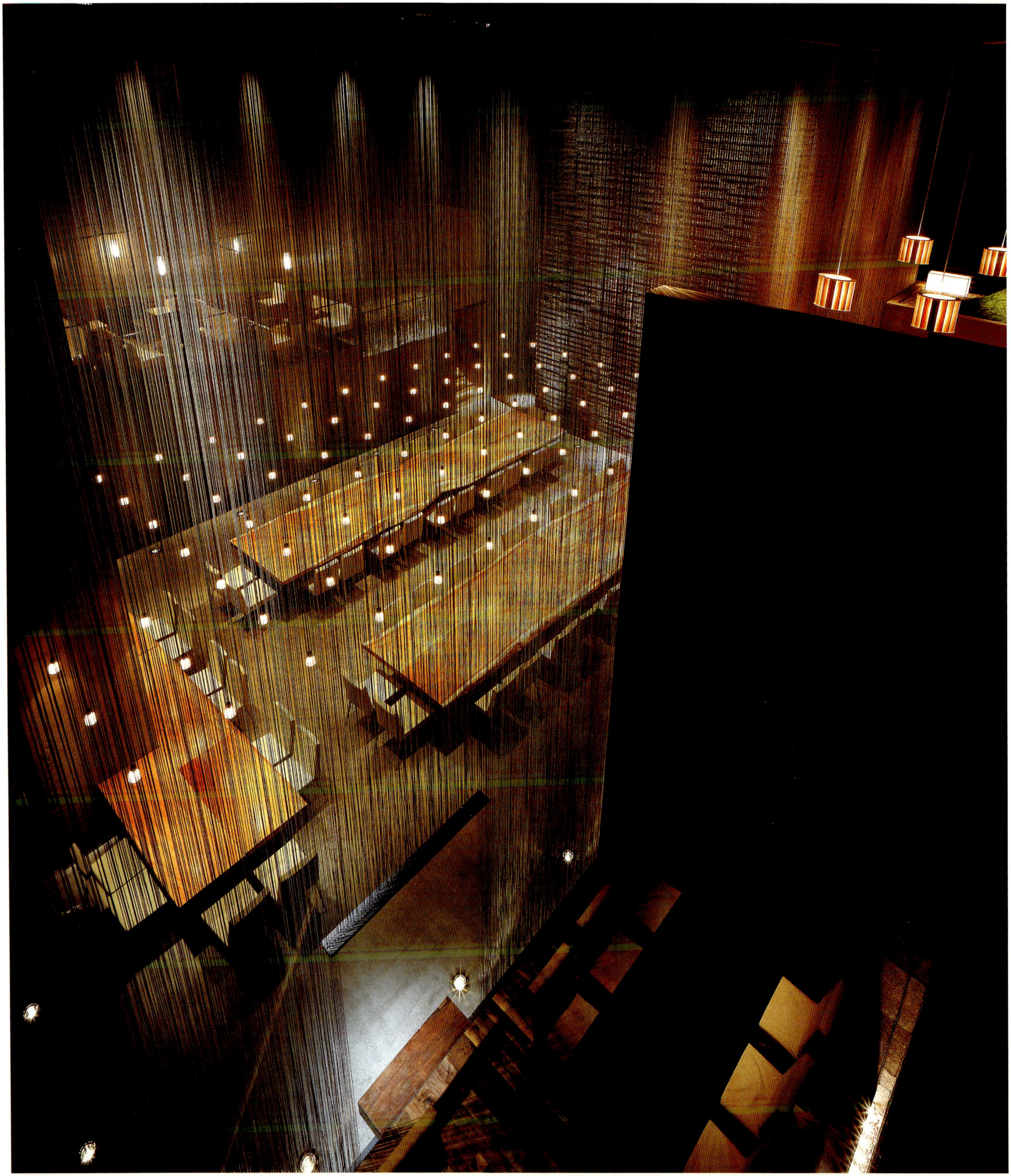

東京

音音

Otooto

Floating worlds under one roof

Formerly a beer house, Otooto's towering interior with its nine-metre high ceiling seemed to have too much space, even for a restaurant. For designer Ryu Kosaka, finding adequate partitions of that height to compose a cosy and comfortable interior was particularly difficult. He looked towards the Ukiyoe or "Floating World", an artistic movement that occurred in urban centres like Tokyo and Kyoto during the Edo Period, for inspiration. He found it in "Rain" by Ando Hiroshige, one of the most famous Ukiyoe artists, who used delicate long black lines vertically oriented to beautifully symbolise heavy rain. Kosaka's idea was to hang coating wires vertically from the nine-metre high ceiling to the ground, creating an astonishing effect. The interior gained much more perspective through this vertical flow.

An open kitchen was built near the entrance area to form a lively, energetic space, in contrast with the centre of the restaurant, where its calm space is spectacularly contrasted with the dramatic rain effect. Otooto's interior encapsulates the Japanese aesthetics of delicacy and dynamism in one space.

FLOORPLAN

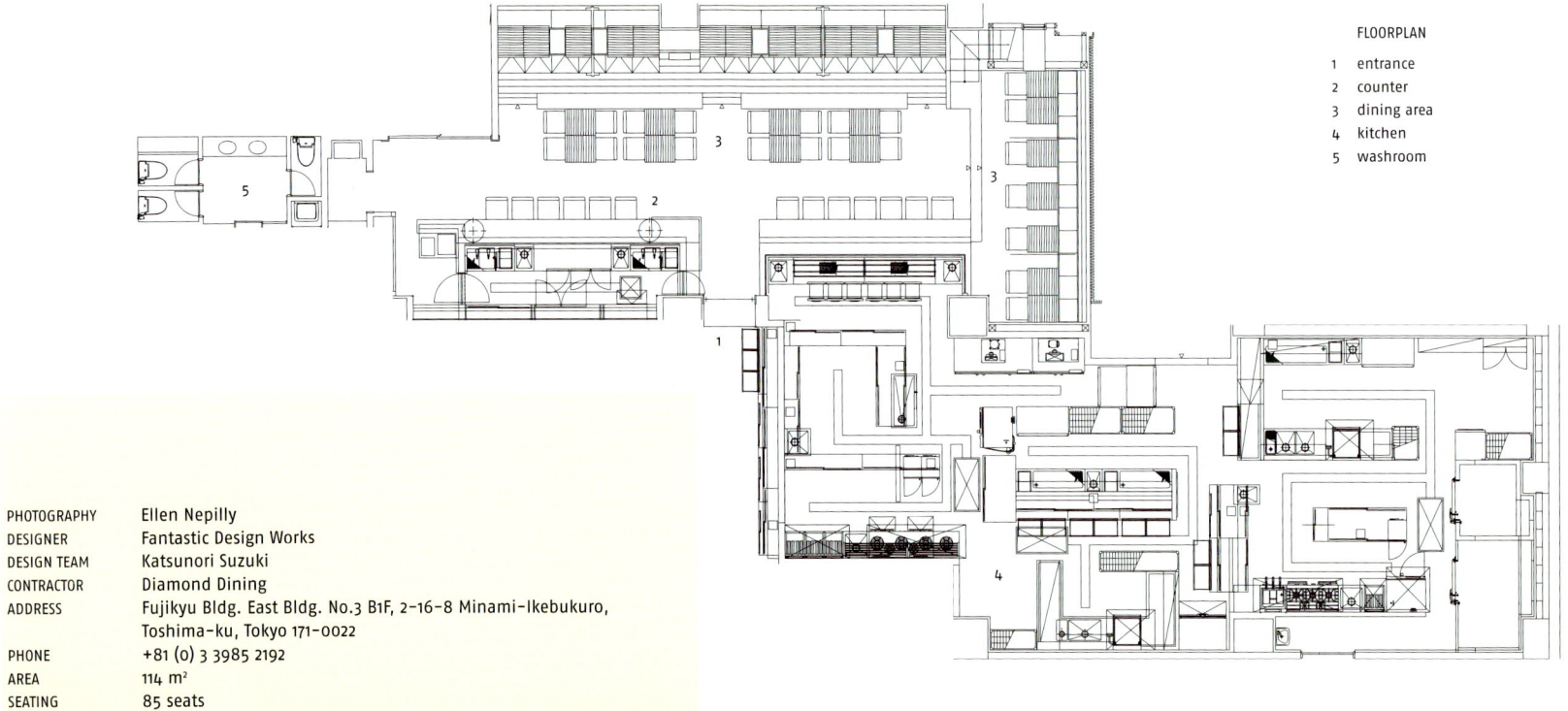

1. entrance
2. counter
3. dining area
4. kitchen
5. washroom

PHOTOGRAPHY	Ellen Nepilly
DESIGNER	Fantastic Design Works
DESIGN TEAM	Katsunori Suzuki
CONTRACTOR	Diamond Dining
ADDRESS	Fujikyu Bldg. East Bldg. No.3 B1F, 2-16-8 Minami-Ikebukuro, Toshima-ku, Tokyo 171-0022
PHONE	+81 (0) 3 3985 2192
AREA	114 m²
SEATING	85 seats
COMPLETED	2005

素材の魅力を表現する愛嬌あふれる空。

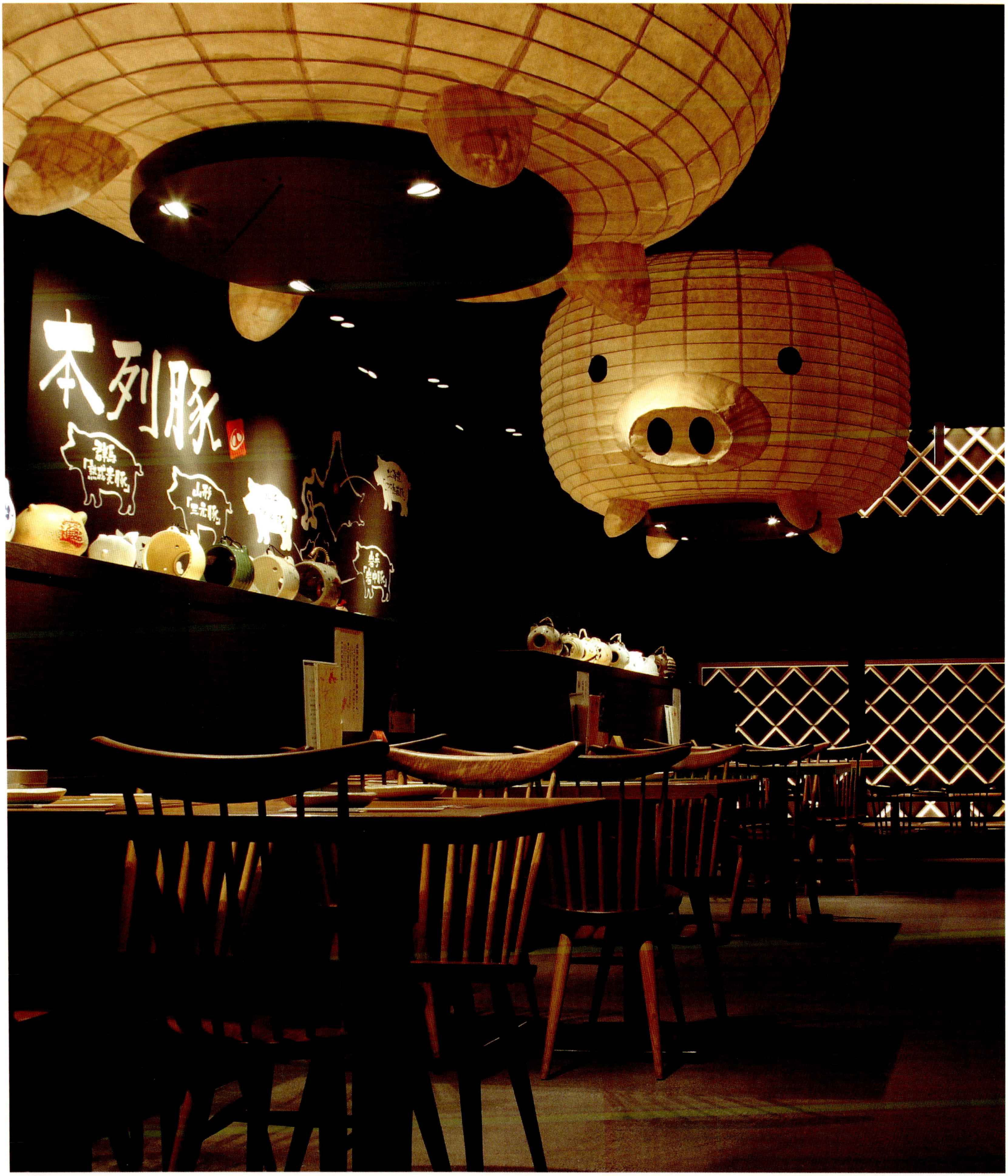

本列豚
群馬「熟成麦豚」
山形「三元豚」
岩手「岩中豚」

東京

三年ぶた蔵

San Nen Buta-zo
Porky paradise

The name San Nen Buta-zo is derived from San Nen Netaro, a famous Japanese children's story about a lazy young man who slept all day for three years. Inspired by the titular character Netaro, designer Katsunori Suzuki chose Buta-zo, a combination of the characters for pig and storage, for the theme of the restaurant. The wall pattern at the back of the restaurant resembles the façade of traditional Japanese kura or zo (storehouses).

San Nen Buta-zo is also famous for its two piggy paper lanterns, uniquely manufactured for the restaurant by Suzuki and probably the biggest of its kind in the world. He started with a simple design, gradually adding a nose, curly tail and little feet, creating possibly the funniest paper lantern hanging in any restaurant. Images of pigs can be found all over the restaurant, from the cute piggy anti-mosquito incense holders on the partitioning wall, to the menu holders designed in the form of pig snouts.

The restaurant offers pork specialties from all over Japan. A special map of Japan, drawn in white on a black wall, shows the different locations from which each pork specialty originates. Typically, the map of Japan with all its islands is called Nihon Retto (the Japanese chain of Islands); on this special map, Suzuki replaces the character for islands with that for pork, giving us a map that clearly illustrates all you need to know about the "Japanese chain of pork".

素材と担い手が共演する、食の円形劇場。

PHOTOGRAPHY	Nacasa & Partners Inc.
DESIGNER	café co.
DESIGN TEAM	Yoshiyuki Morii
CONTRACTOR	Food Scope, inc.
ADDRESS	Herbis ENT 5F 2-2-22 Umeda Kita-ku, Osaka 530-0001
PHONE	+81 (0) 6 6456 2388
AREA	250 m²
SEATING	100 seats, 4 private rooms
COMPLETED	2004

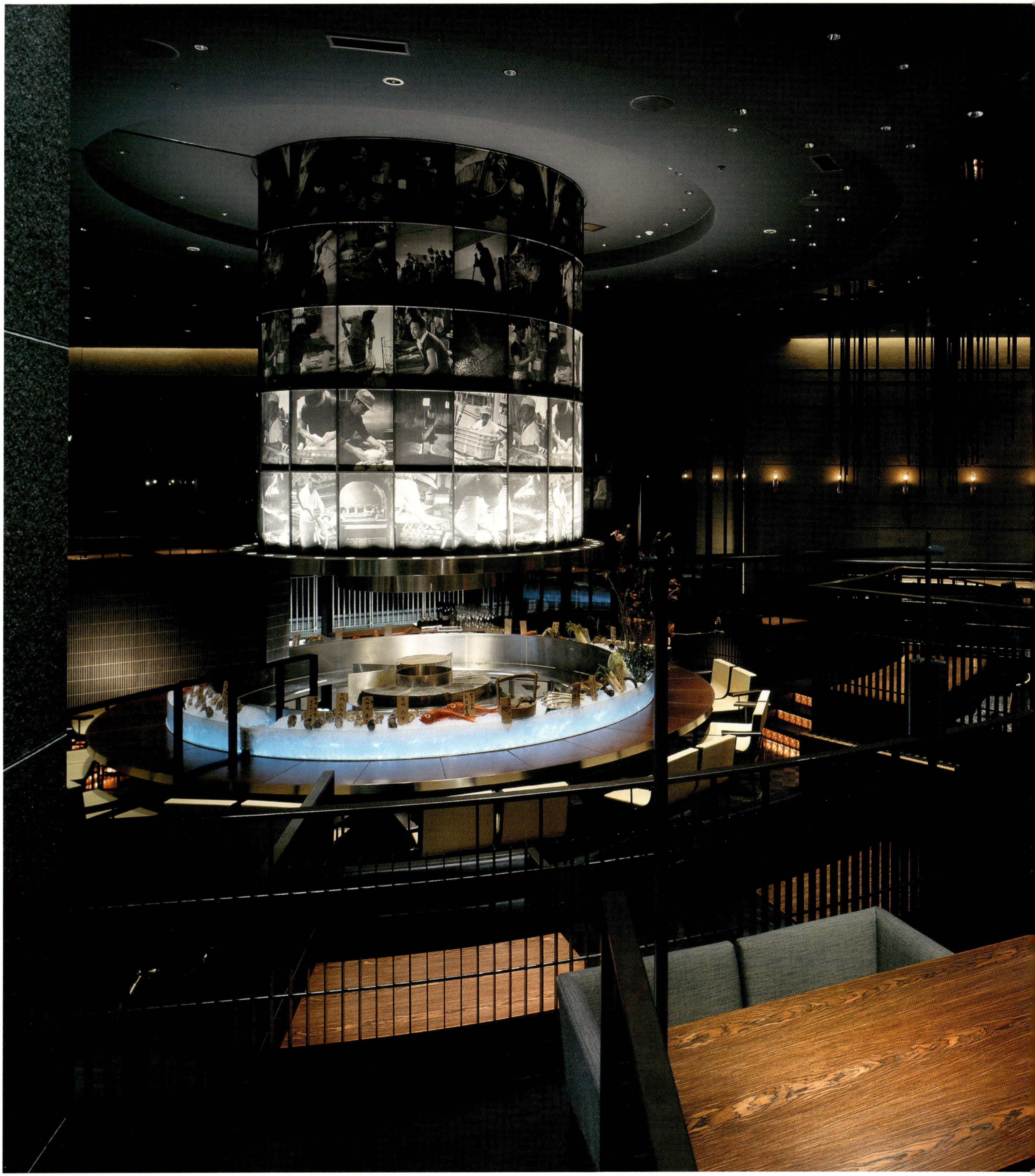

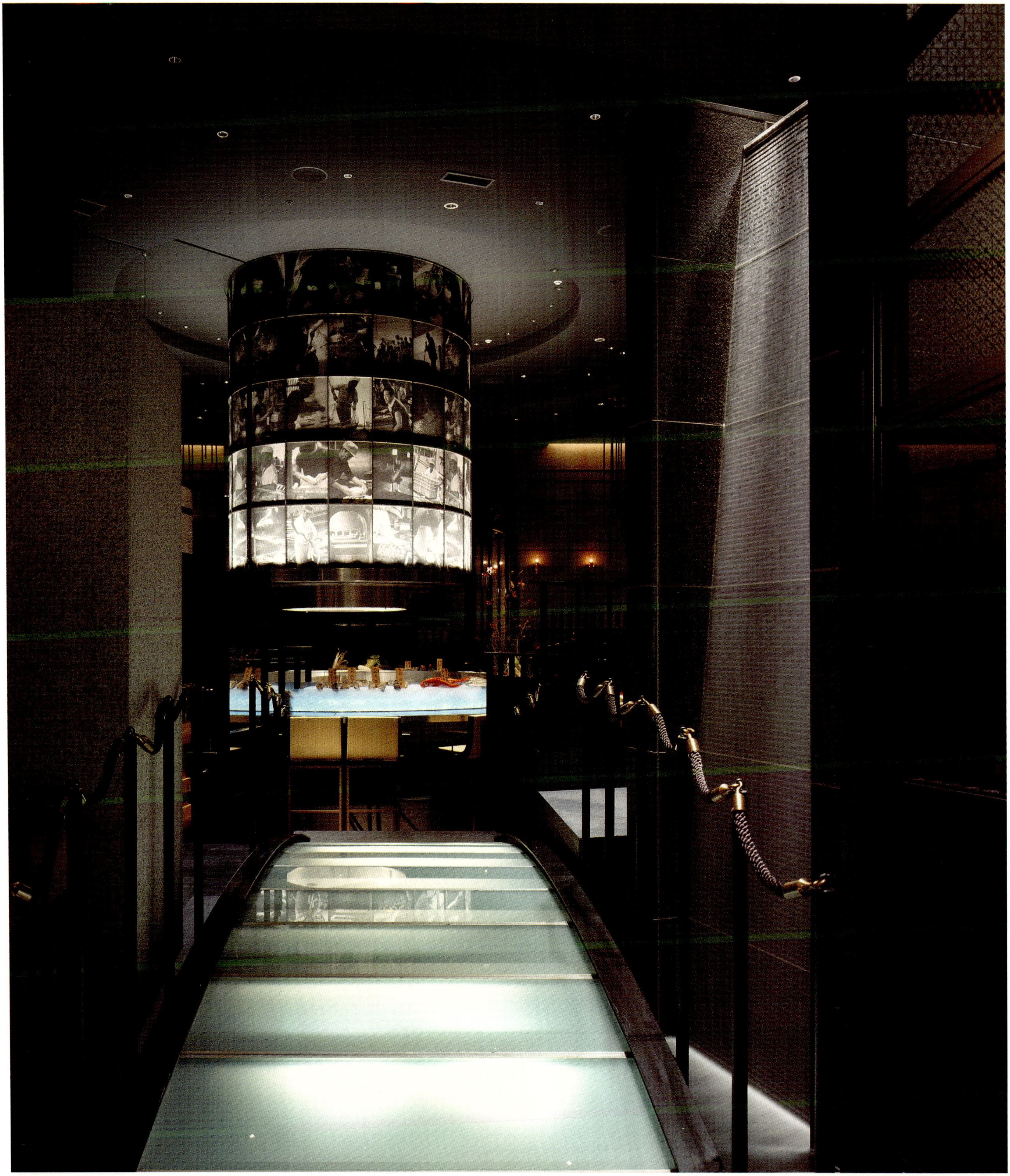

大阪

美食米門

Bishoku Maimon

Dining in a grand arena

The first thing that guests at Bishoku Maimon will notice even before stepping into its premises is the little arching bridge within leading into the main dining hall. Paved with frosted blue glass and illuminated from beneath, the bridge is quite the beauty. However, the restaurant's real highlight is a spectacular ice counter that displays a glorious array of fresh delicacies. With cool blue light under the ice counter complementing the natural dark colours of the restaurant's interior, the result is aesthetic brilliance.

Designer Yoshiyuki Morii's idea was to create a food stadium, with the counter serving as the focal point of attention. From the tables arranged in ascending tiers all around, guests can enjoy a panoramic view of the chefs preparing food and admire the luminous black and white photographs displayed above the counter. The images depict Japanese fishermen, tofu makers and other workers from food-related professions. To make the main dining hall seem less cavernous, thin dark poles are carefully hung from the high ceiling in different lengths around the counter. The design of the private rooms is just as intriguing, albeit somewhat reminiscent of cosy dungeons.

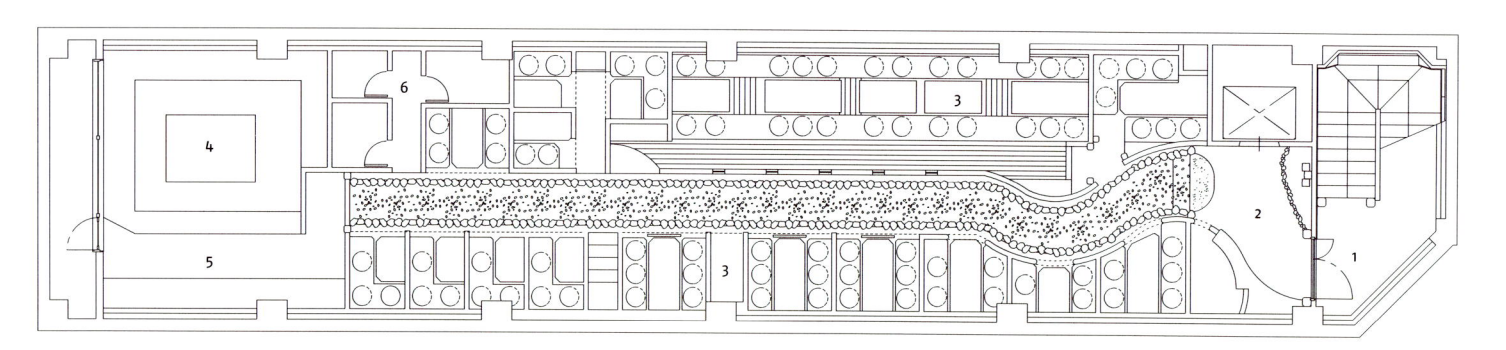

FLOORPLAN

1. entrance
2. reception
3. dining area
4. kitchen
5. pantry
6. washroom

PHOTOGRAPHY	Ellen Nepilly
DESIGNER	Tamo Design & Engineering
DESIGN TEAM	Masaru Sagara
CONTRACTOR	Meal System
ADDRESS	1-13-1 Taguliet Ikebukuro B1F, Nishi-Ikebukuro, Nerima-ku, Tokyo 171-0021
PHONE	+81 (0) 3 5949 5885
AREA	126 m²
SEATING	87 seats
COMPLETED	2004

八百万の神が宿る古の家に抱かれる心地よさ。

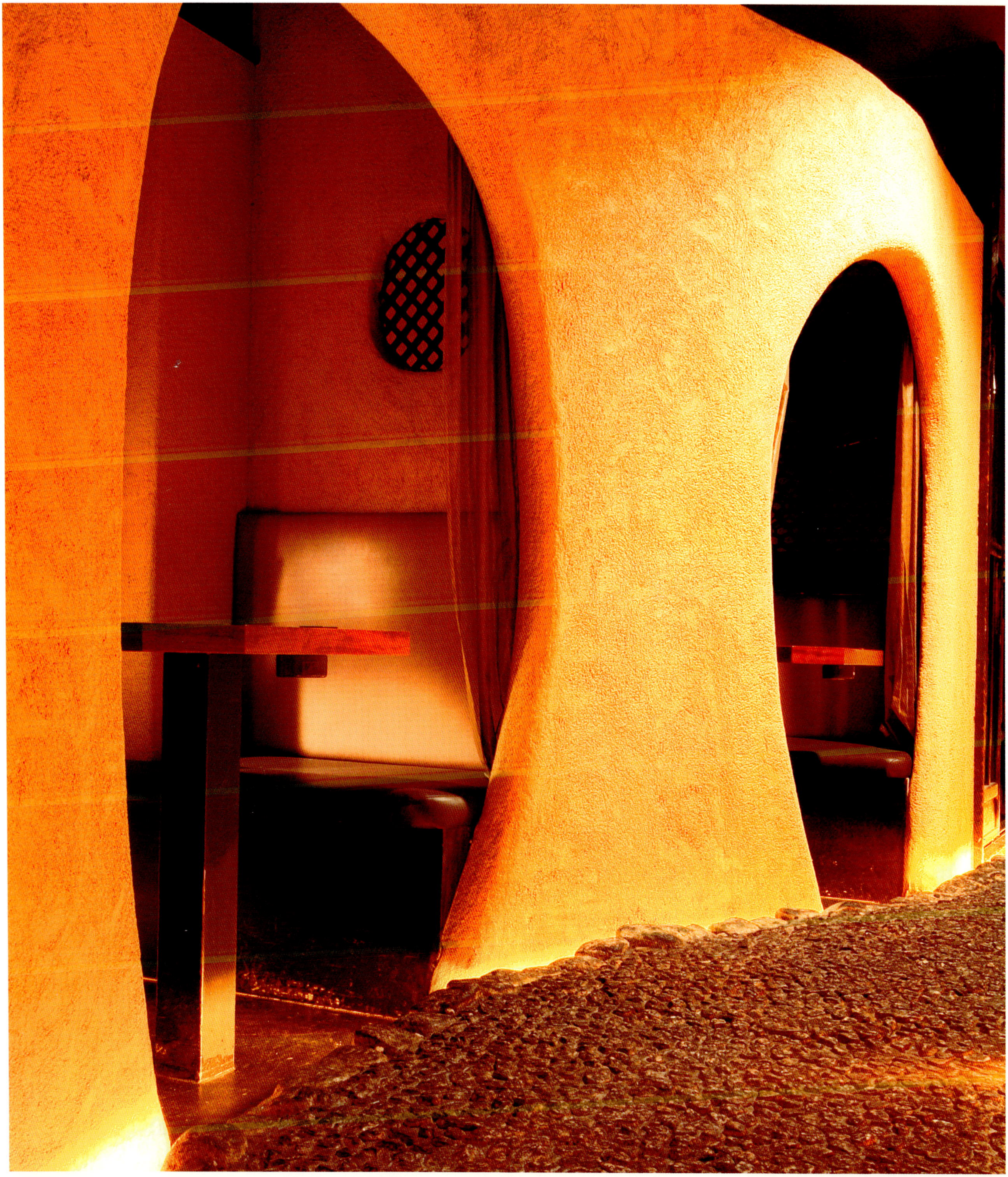

東京

さいぞう

Saizo

Earthen comforts in urban corners

In the huge buzzing city of Tokyo where there are few places to be alone, restaurants such as Saizo offer the rare comfort of privacy. Guests can retreat into its private cubicles and secluded dining areas. In areas like Ikebukuro that are teeming with companies, businessmen seek daily refuge at restaurants like Saizo, which offer the perfect place to dine with colleagues or customers after work, or before embarking on the long train ride home.

Designer Masaru Sagara used mainly wood and natural materials for the interior. The pillars, girders, sliding doors, and furniture in the rear of the restaurant were transported from an old private traditional house. For the surface of the walls, a mixture of straw and diatomaceous Earth was applied, giving both sides of the hallway the look and feel of a gravel road, while warm, indirect light added to the cosy atmosphere of the organic interior.

At the back of the restaurant, there is a sitting area with glass flooring under which you can see water gently flowing through to a small Japanese garden. Other elevated levels can be accessed by a flight of wooden stairs. One of the bigger rooms serves as a private function room for company parties and roller blinds can be added or detached, depending on the size of the group. Like many restaurants in Japan, a nomihodai menu is offered, where guests pay a certain amount to drink as much as they want within a certain time frame. In the Japanese business world, the importance of drinking cannot be underestimated.

FIRST FLOOR

1 entrance
2 dining area
3 kitchen
4 bar
5 washroom

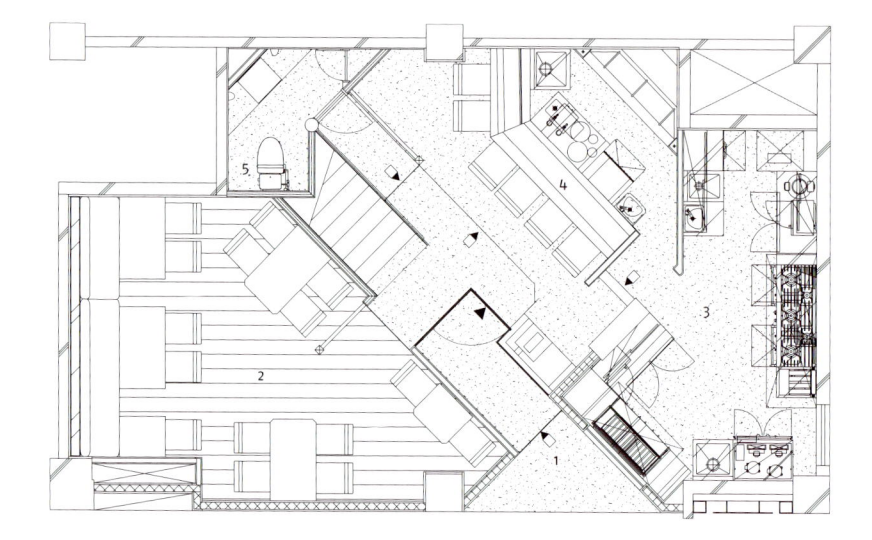

SECOND FLOOR

1 entrance
2 dining area
3 kitchen
4 washroom

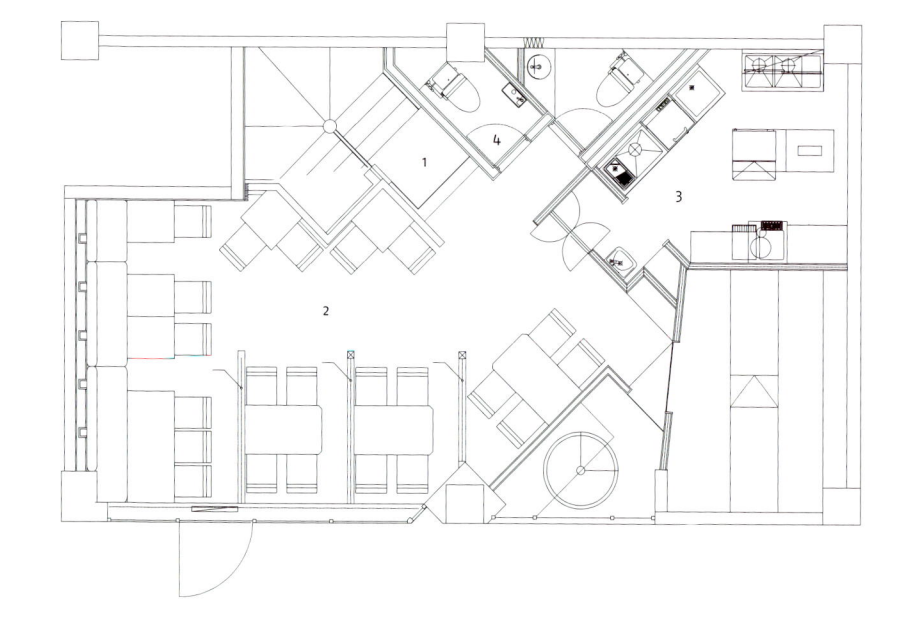

PHOTOGRAPHY	Hiroshi Tsujitani (Nacasa & Partners Inc.)
DESIGNER	Descartes Inc.
DESIGN TEAM	Takumi Sato, Katsuhiko Yamamoto
CONTRACTOR	Shitamachi co., ltd.
ADDRESS	Shitamachi Bldg. 1F, 4-28-2 Kotobashi, Sumida-ku, Tokyo 130-0022
PHONE	+81 (0) 3 3633 7473
AREA	132 m²
SEATING	66 seats
COMPLETED	2006

和の紋様と感性が、集う人を寛容に包み込む。

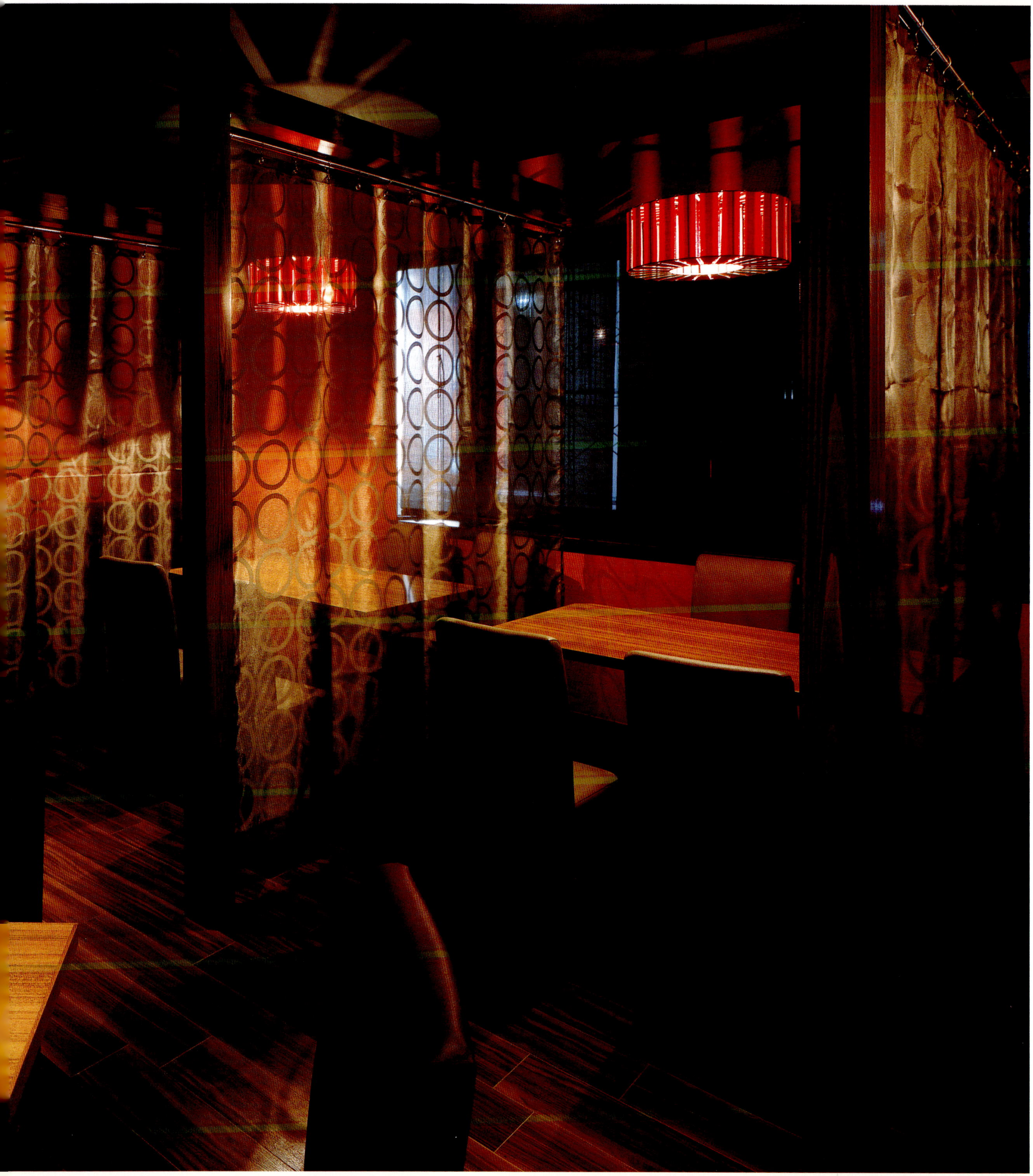

東京

器

Utsuwa

A modern twist to tradition

Utsuwa is located in the established part of downtown Tokyo, where traditional restaurants prevail. Designers Katsuhiko Yamamoto and Takumi Sato were given the brief of creating a different - but not over the top - interior and façade.

Directly facing commuters coming out of the station, Utsuwa makes the most of its site advantage with an interesting and inviting façade. The designers used conventional Japanese patterns in contemporary shades, giving a modern twist to traditional Japanese styles. These graphic patterns are printed on panels and mounted onto the storefront. Another interesting feature which attracts the curiosity of passersby is the little storefront window that peeks into the triangular kitchen framing the chef in action.

Inside the restaurant, the designers creatively lined the fabric-covered feature wall with Japanese sliding door handles. The use of traditional elements on the elegant silver-grey background reflects a clever use of material that is economical and forms a contrast to the facing wall wallpapered in a purple Western pattern. On the second floor, sheer curtains partition the semi-private seating areas; the privacy adds a comfortable and relaxing touch to the dining experience.

The designers customised the lamps especially for Utsuwa. The most outstanding has to be the brilliant red creation of cleverly bound inverted champagne glasses.

天空の煌めきを封じ込め、今宵ひと時を楽しむ。

PHOTOGRAPHY	Ellen Nepilly
DESIGNER	Atta Co., Ltd.
DESIGN TEAM	Akihide Toida
CONTRACTOR	Enterprise Huge co., Ltd.
ADDRESS	Mikomoto Ginza 2 8F/9F, Ginza 2-4-12, Chuo-ku, Tokyo 104-0061
PHONE	+81 (0) 3 5159 0991
AREA	392 m²
SEATING	120 seats, 2 private rooms
COMPLETED	2006

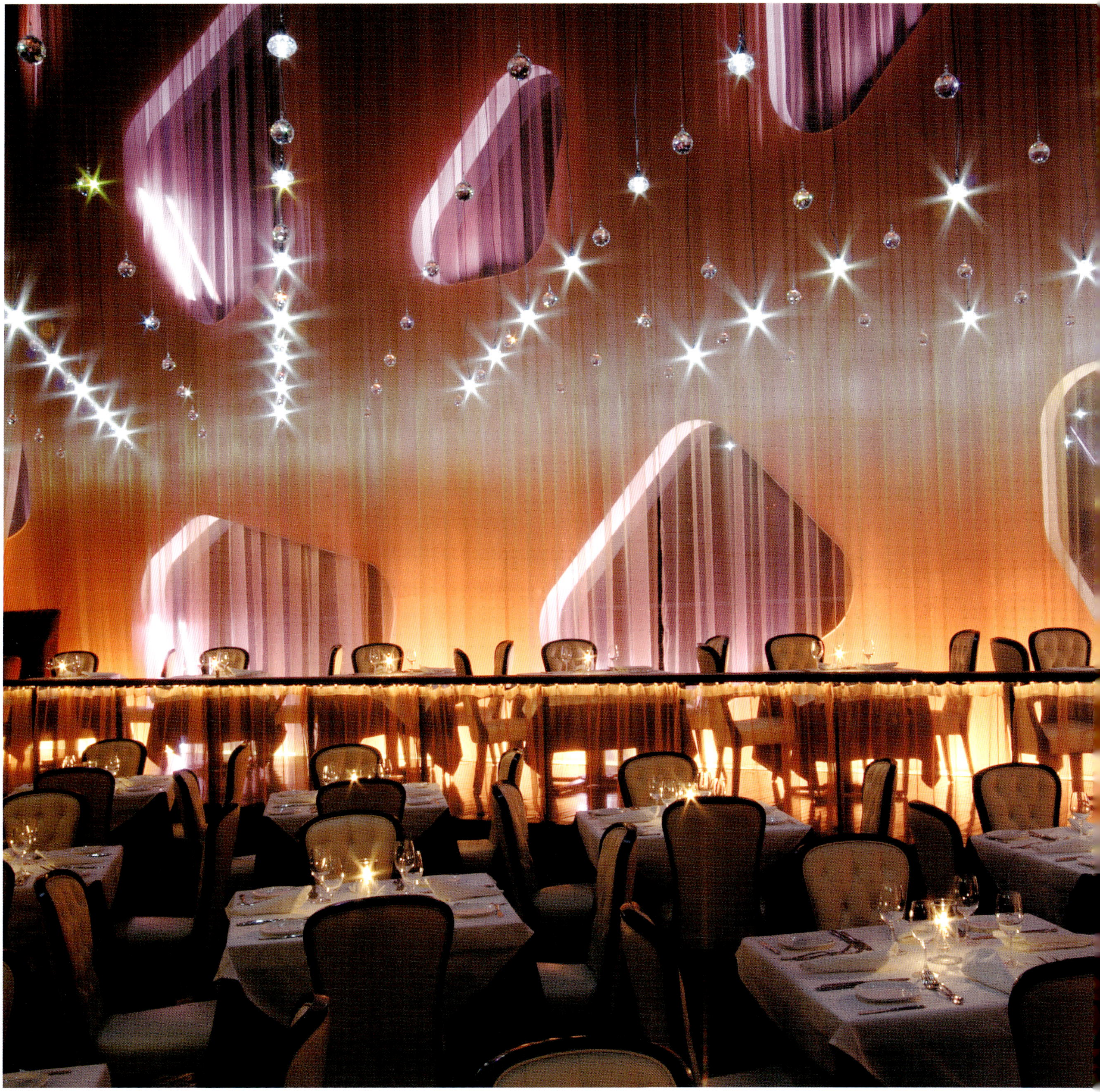

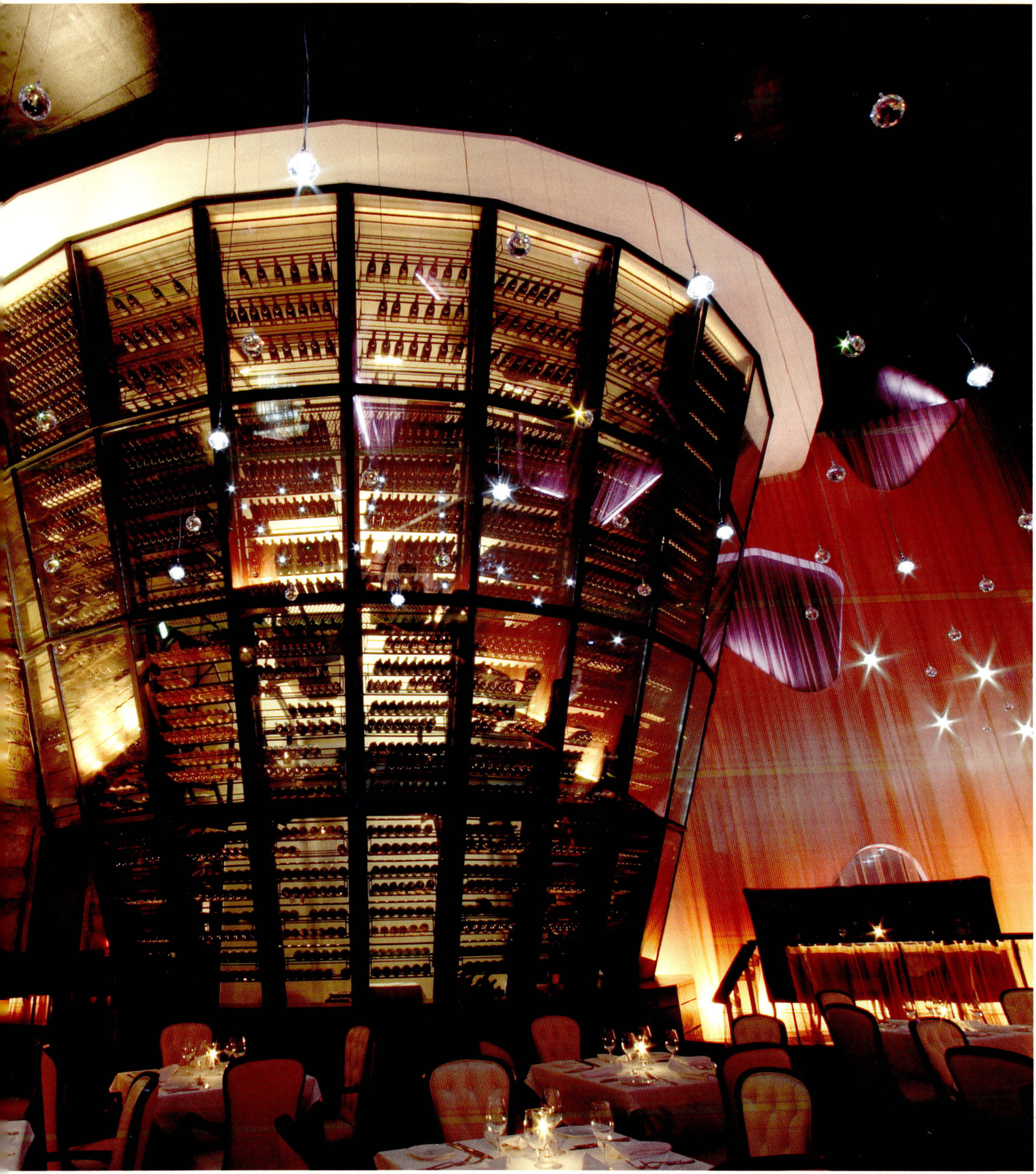

東京

ダズル

Dazzle

Dazzling

Located on the eighth and ninth floor of the second Mikimoto building in Ginza, Dazzle is exactly as it claims. Stepping out of the main elevator, which stops on the eighth floor, guests find themselves in the company of chefs, right in the middle of the action of the open kitchen. Before they stop to wonder if they have arrived at the wrong place, a friendly waiter is already on his way to lead guests either to the bar or the other elevator that services the ninth floor, where the actual restaurant is situated. The service here is as impressive as the interior.

Dazzle has the right mix. It is posh without being too extravagant. Apricot, orange and purple hues form a mixture of rustic elegance and luxury creating a spectacular atmosphere. Suspended lighting, Swarovski crystal balls, sheer curtains and deluxe chairs are details that give the restaurant its special touch. There is even a wall, which reminds guests of textured stonewalls in ancient European castles. The outlines of the signature blobbed openings of the building, designed by architect Toyo Ito, is allowed to shine through the sheer curtains. The ceiling is a mesmerising sea of 170 shimmering Swarovski crystals and lighting that alternate in orderly rows, suspended above the space.

The most outstanding feature is the inverted cone that displays up to 3,500 bottles of wine. Diagonally arranging the room, designer Akihide Toida manages to create the illusion of a larger room that dazzles the eye.

023

悦楽優、すべてを包み込む手鞠の世界。

PHOTOGRAPHY	Hirokazu Matsuoka
DESIGNER	calm.design co., ltd.
DESIGN TEAM	Takuya Kanazawa
CONTRACTOR	Diamond Dining
ADDRESS	HMX Pavilion Bldg. 5F, 3-28-10 Sinjyuku, Sinjyuku-ku, Tokyo 160-0022
PHONE	+81 (0) 3 3226 8070
AREA	212 m²
SEATING	120 seats, 17 private rooms
COMPLETED	2006

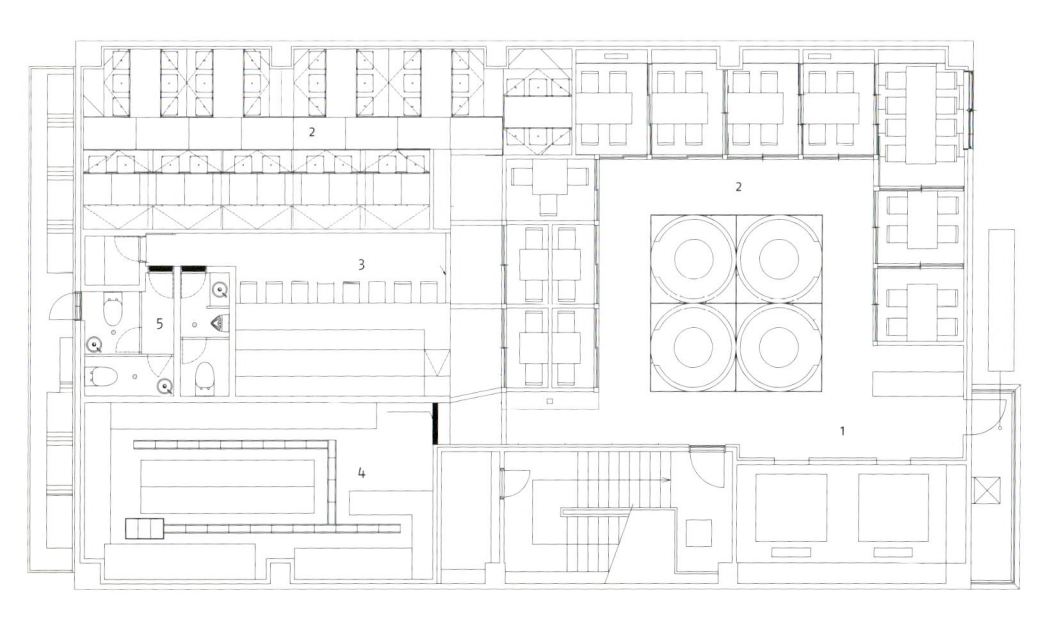

FLOORPLAN

1 entrance
2 dining area
3 bar
4 kitchen
5 washroom

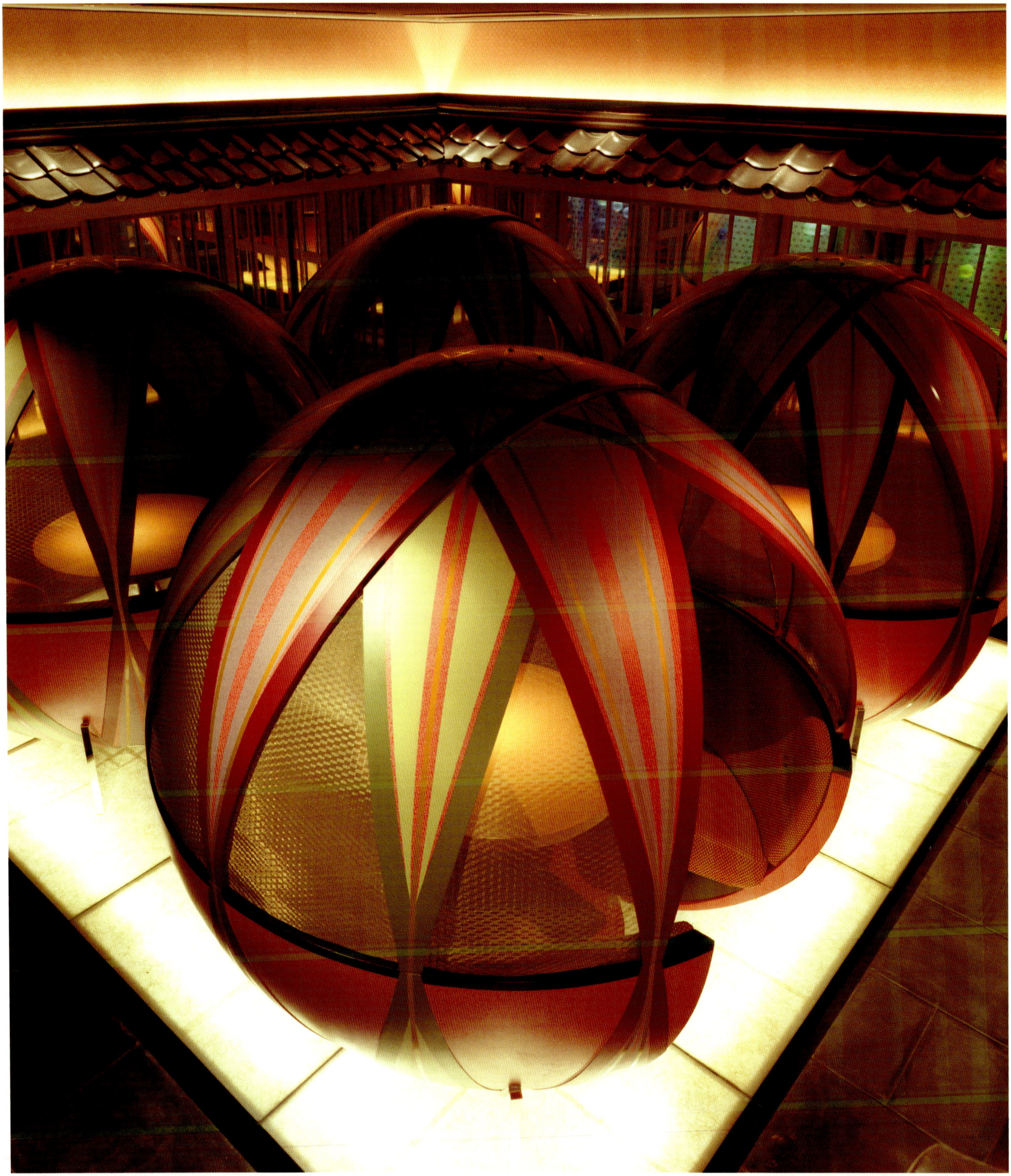

東京

七色てまりうた

Nanairo Temariuta

Namesake toy from bygone eras

First created in the Heian Period, the temari was popularised during the Edo period as a game to pass time. These colourful handmade fabric balls, often in silk, were attached to the hand, and played with. Today the beautifully crafted balls form a part of Japanese art and culture.

Located in Shinjuku, one of the liveliest districts of Tokyo, the interior of sushi restaurant Nanairo Temariuta features its namesake toy from bygone eras. At the heart of the premise is a dining area where four giant temari balls stand. Each ball sits up to six guests, who dine in exclusivity. Guests sit comfortably on a bench encircling the small table.

These oversized temaris in rainbow colours are raised on a lit platform. White floor lighting highlights the structures and makes them the centre of attention. The contrasting black floor tiling further enhances the illuminated pedestal. The surrounding rooms emulate buildings of an ancient Edo castle town. Each dining section is unique, creating spaces that interweave the stillness of the Heian Period and the activeness of the Edo Period.

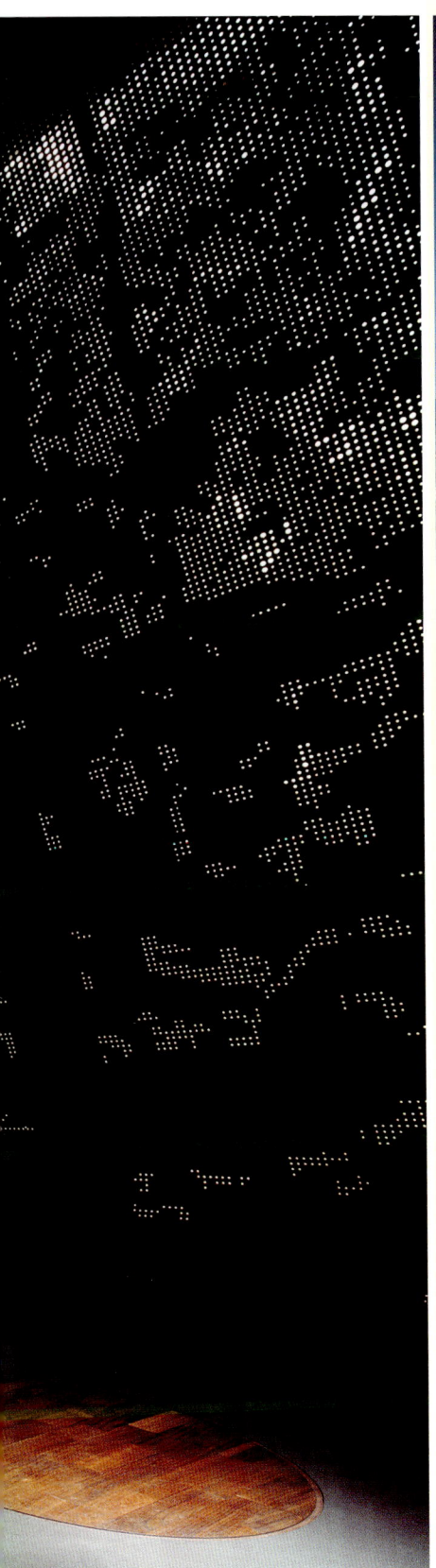

PHOTOGRAPHY	Daici Ano
DESIGNER	Hitoshi Abe + Atelier Hitoshi Abe
DESIGN TEAM	Naoki Inada, Yasuyuki Sakuma
CONTRACTOR	Dateno Gyutan co., ltd.
ADDRESS	2-13-21 Kokubuncho, Aoba-ku, Sendai City, Miyagi 980-0803
PHONE	+81 (0) 2 2716 6761
AREA	220 m²
SEATING	28 seats
COMPLETED	2006

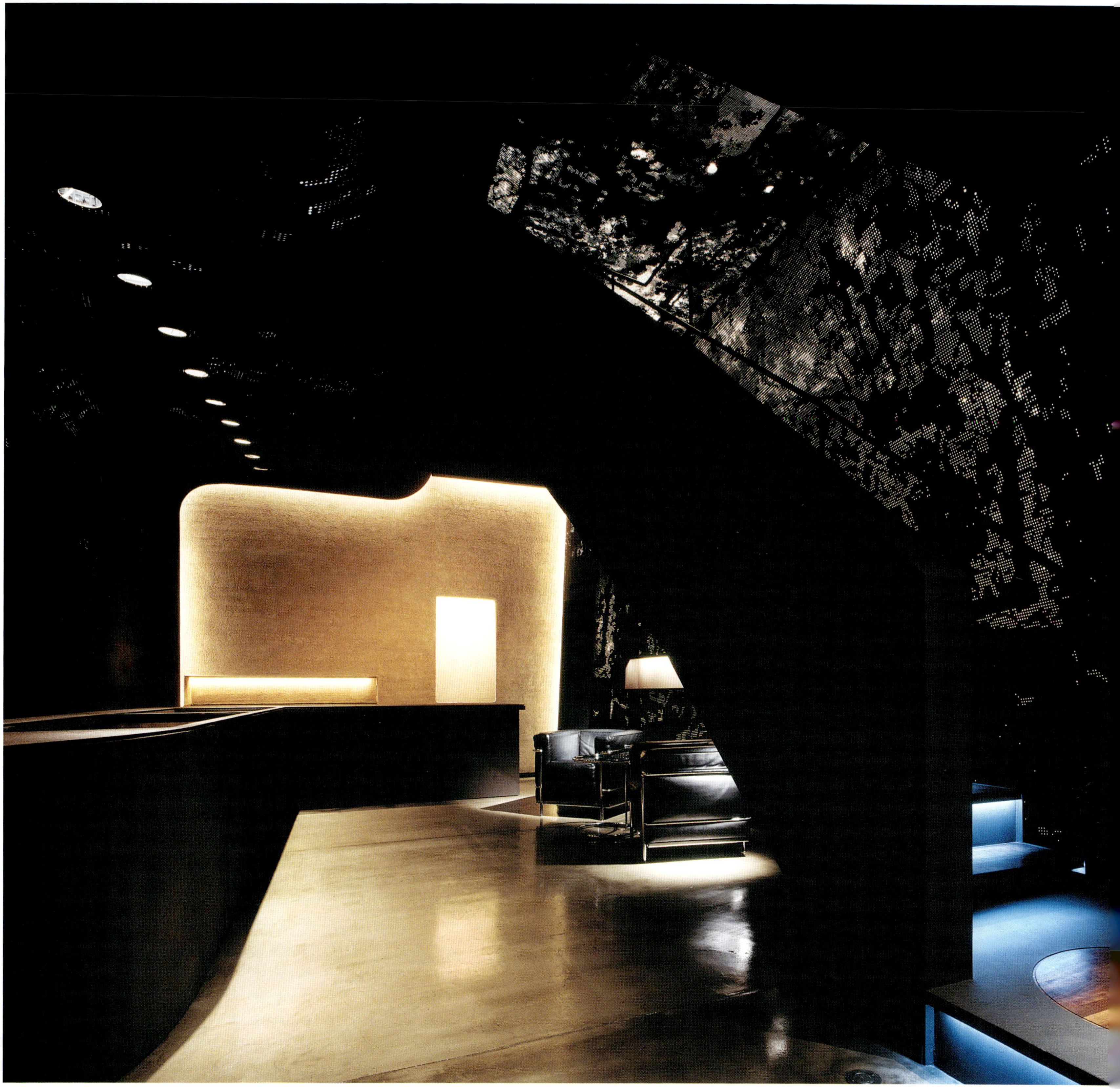

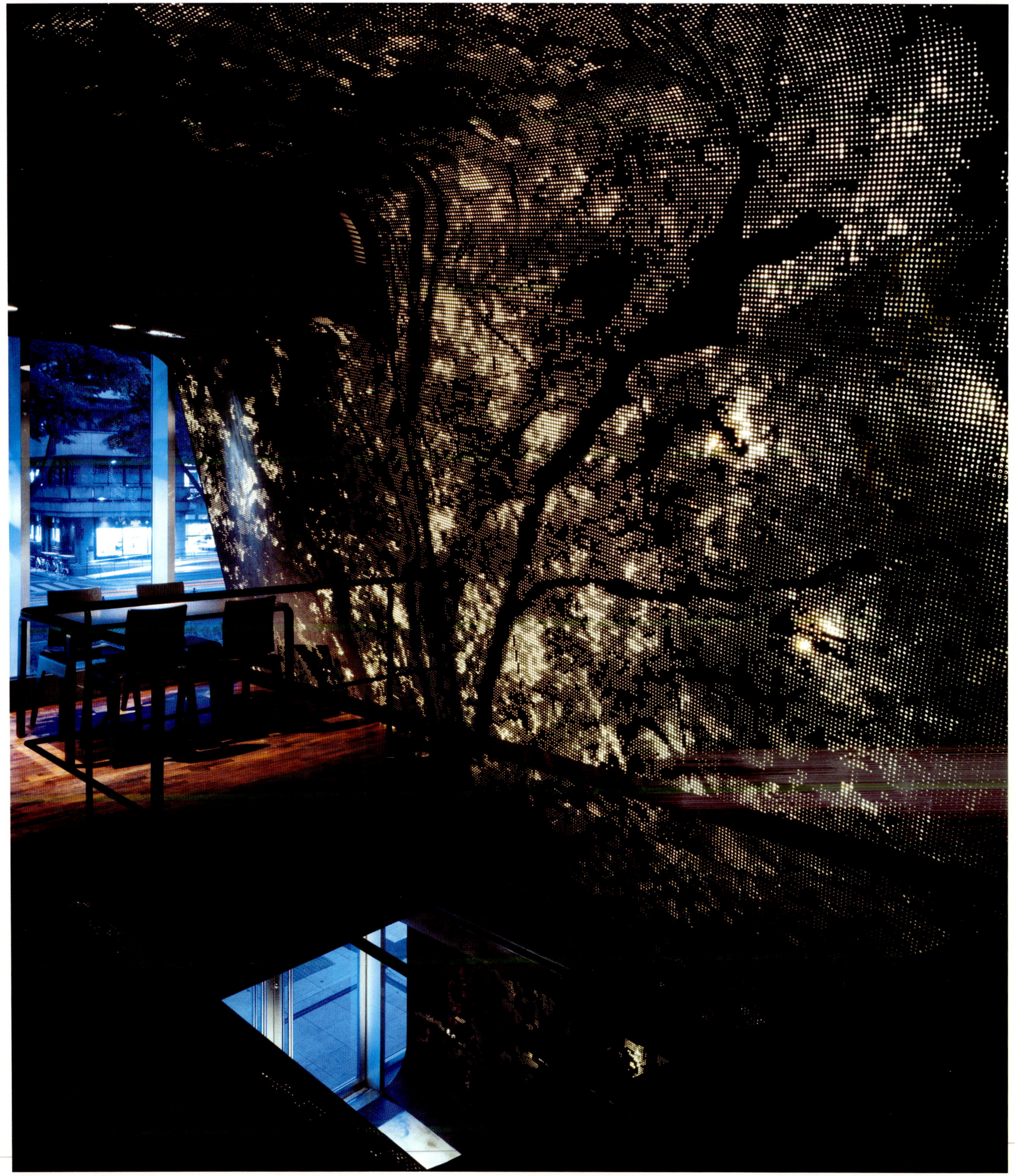

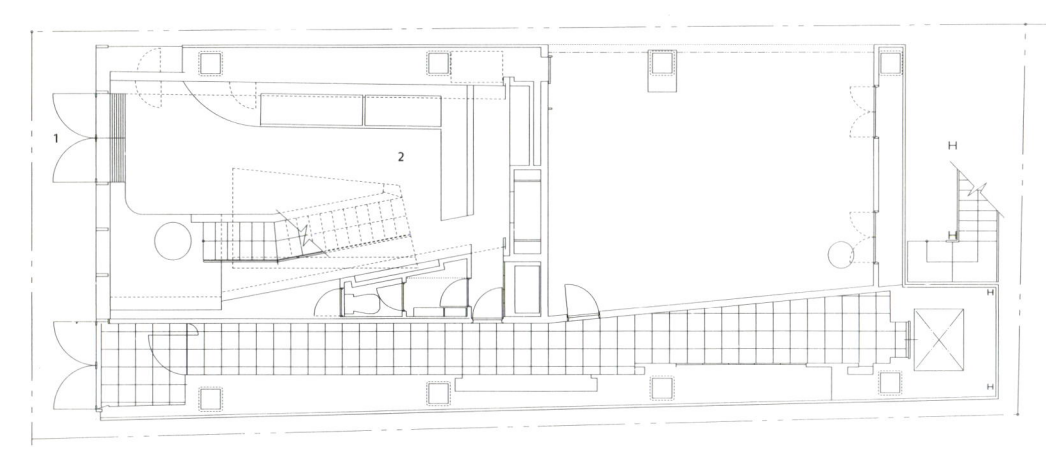

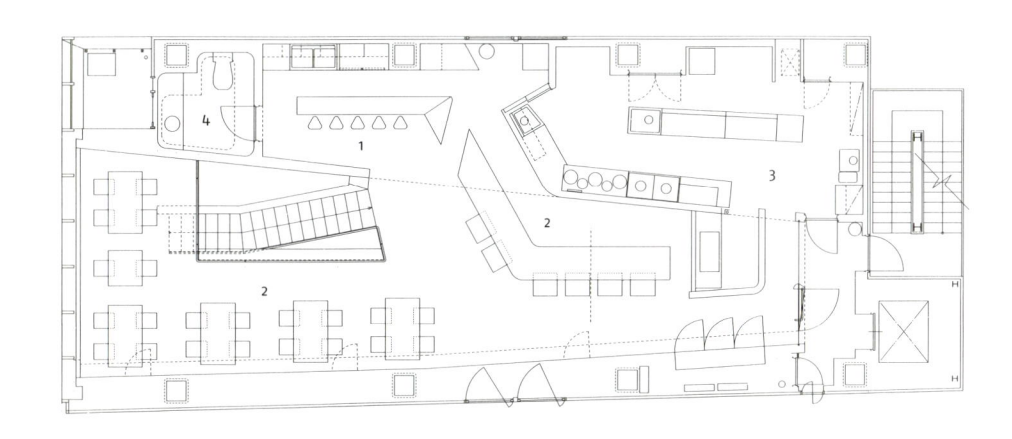

FIRST FLOOR
1. entrance
2. reception

SECOND FLOOR
1. bar
2. dining area
3. kitchen
4. washroom

まるで闇を手懐けるような、妖艶を放つ異空間。

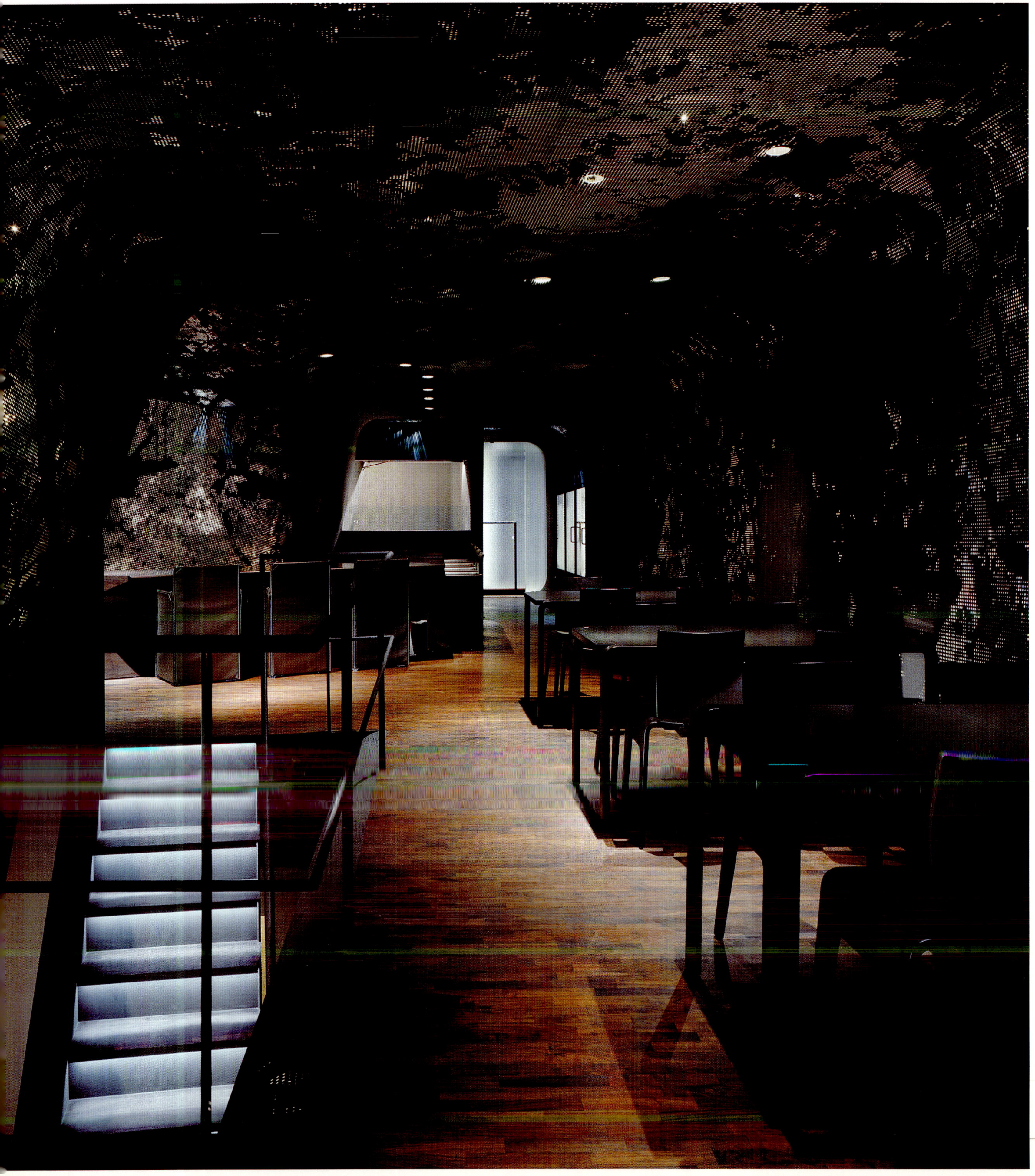

仙台

青葉亭

Aoba-Tei

Illuminated Zelkova trees

Aoba-Tei, a French restaurant in Sendai, faces the famous Jozenji Street. About two hours north of Tokyo by Shinkansen, Sendai is the capital of Miyagi prefecture. It is fondly nicknamed the City of Trees after its famous Zelkova tree-lined streets.

The restaurant features a ribbon of steel that is bent to form secondary inner walls stretching from the first to the second floor. The steel ribbon forms two inverted conical funnels lying on their sides, one on top of the other. The funnel tapers on the second floor to frame the view of the street lined by the beautiful Zelkova trees.

The steel plate itself is perforated with tiny holes of assorted sizes. Backlighting filters through to reveal Zelkova tree patterns. The illumination creates a stunning and magical interior.

What appears to be a continuous steel ribbon was actually delivered in pieces that could fit through the entrance and welded on the spot. Back illumination made the welding work tricky as the tiniest of cracks and holes could be easily spotted. Thereafter, architect Hitoshi Abe assigned a specialist in ship steel welding to take on the precision work.

PHOTOGRAPHY	Masahiro Ishibashi
DESIGNER	Zoukei Syudan Co.,Ltd.
DESIGN TEAM	Yusaku Kaneshiro, Miho Umeda
CONTRACTOR	Ryukyu Communication
ADDRESS	Okinawa-Suntory Building 2F, 2-1-15 Matsuyama, Naha City, Okinawa 900-0032
PHONE	+81 (0) 9 8941 0232
AREA	244 m²
SEATING	124 seats
COMPLETED	2004

龍神が誘う、冒険と空想に満たされた時。

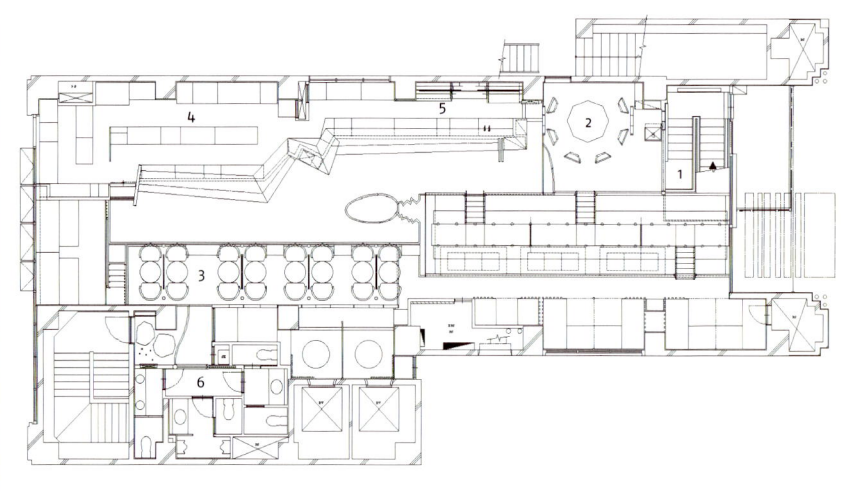

FLOORPLAN

1 entrance
2 reception
3 dining area
4 kitchen
5 bar
6 washroom

010

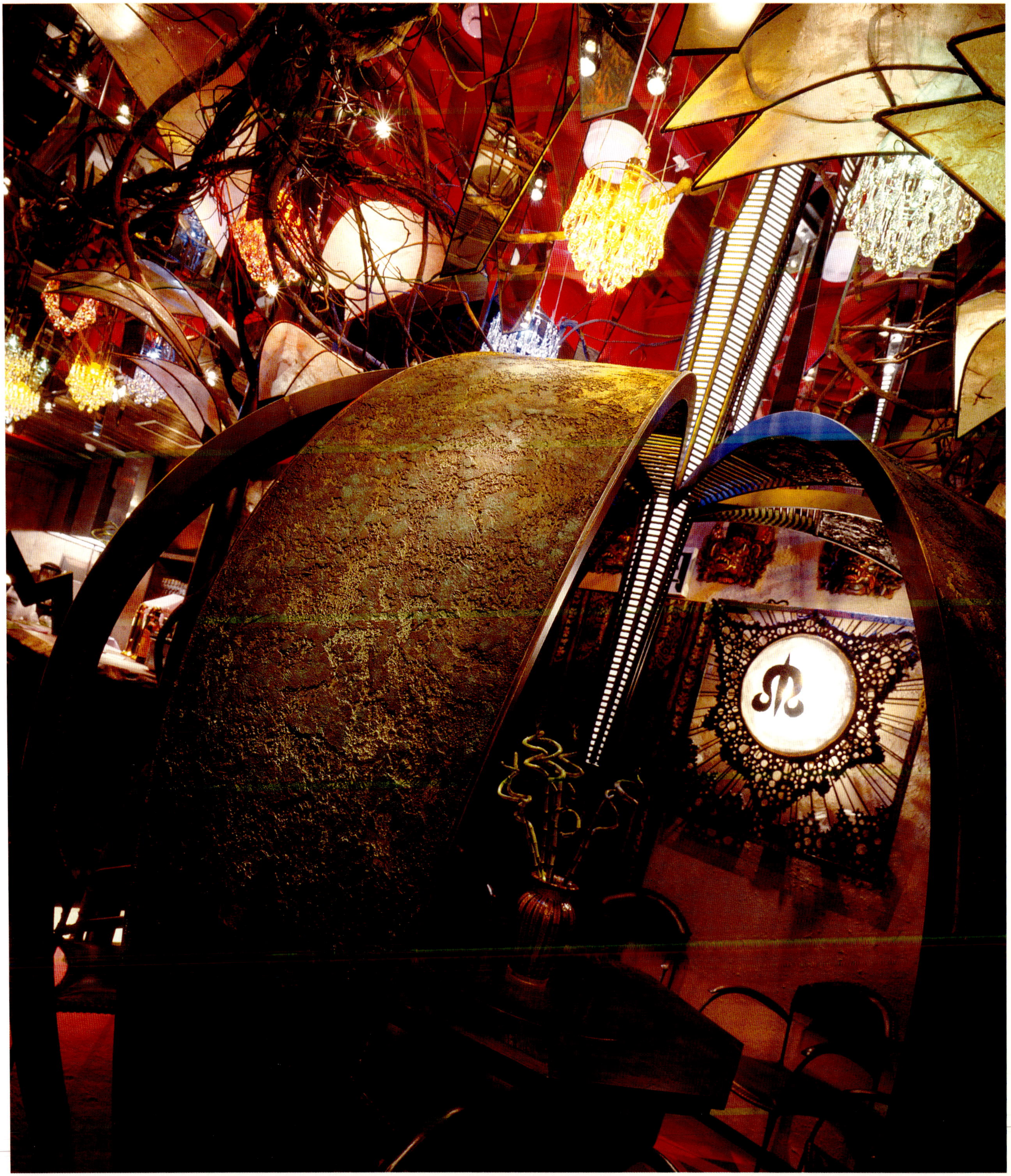

沖縄

タイタイ

Thai Thai Okinawa

Cavorting with fire breathing dragons

The oval shaped sign above the entrance of this Okinawan restaurant in downtown Naha claims to offer exotic asian dining. In effect, not only is the food exotic, so is the design of the restaurant. What looks like an elaborate construction to hold an illuminated sign is actually a tubular structure that houses seats for the guests. The interior could be the set of a fantasy movie, where the tube is the space ship that has just lowered its stairs for disembarkation. Inside the tube, a warm golden brown hue makes guests feel comfortable and protected. Cavorting below, on raked sand, are dragons looking as if they are about to breath fire. Each of the dragons are crafted in Bali and assembled on-site, the largest of which measures 20 m long.

High-backed acrylic seats are the feature of the couples-dining area. The pearly sheen of the acrylic shells gives an ethereal glow to the atmosphere. Semi-transparent glass panels separate the round tables from each other, creating a cozy space for couples to dine in privacy. Enhanced by the warm lighting, the area is intimate and inviting. The ceiling of twisted twigs and tree branches is accessorised with teardrop chandeliers illuminated by different coloured bulbs and mirror fragments. Each of the private dining spaces is designed differently so dining in Thai Thai never gets boring.

HOKKAIDO · SHARI · RAUSO · KUSHIRO · NAMURO

Many people associate Japanese dining with Zen style sushi bars or teriyaki restaurants. However, Japanese dining culture is evidently so much more than that. Not only is there a myriad of different Japanese dishes to savour, there is also a unique diversity of restaurants preparing them. Their number is beyond comparison - it is said that there are more than 80,000 restaurants in Tokyo alone.

In huge cities like Tokyo or Osaka, where many people live in rather tiny apartments, entertaining at home is rare. Thus for special events like birthdays or just a regular get-together with friends, it is more common to dine out. To accommodate groups more comfortably, restaurants started to offer specially designed private rooms.

In the density of Japanese cities where privacy is a rare treat, restaurants that provide secluded private spaces have become increasingly popular in recent years. What attracts most Japanese diners of the younger generation is often not to see and be seen, but rather dining in the cosy atmosphere of an exclusive space that ensures a feeling of privacy. The phenomenon of private rooms appeared after the economic crisis of the '90s. In contrast to the communitarian spirit of their parents, the younger generation increasingly appreciated a sense of individuality. In contrast to the monotony at the workplace, mainly open-plan offices' or long commuting hours in trains packed like sardines in a tin, this younger generation started looking for exclusivity during their private time. The experience of dining in a distinctive atmosphere that designer's restaurants have to offer is one. Being able to retreat to private rooms and secluded corners gives diners a feeling of privilege instead of being one of many. As a result, hip restaurants started to mushroom.

This book introduces different facets of Japanese restaurants with different approaches to make their guests feel special. There are dining booths in the form of tiny houses, semi-private areas partitioned with curtains or blinds, fantastic cabins designed to look like flower buds, and even huge balls in which guests can retreat.

Hip Dining Japan showcases a selection of some of the most extraordinary restaurants Japan has to offer. It does not only introduce stunningly extraordinary restaurant design, but also explains with each chapter different aspects of Japanese culture.

序章 *Introduction*

HAKODATE
MORIAKA
YAMAGATA SENDAI
HONSHU
YAMAGUCHI
HIROSHIMA
KYOTO
OTSU
NAGASAKI
OITA
SHIKOKU
YOKOHAMA TOKYO
CHIBA
KYUSHU
KAGOSHIMA

006	Introduction	104	Ikki
008	Thai Thai Okinawa	108	Robutaya
014	Aoba-Tei	114	Tubomi
020	Nanairo Temariuta	120	The Wizard of the Opera
024	Dazzle	126	Kadoshika
028	Utsuwa	132	Taketori 100 Monogatari
032	Saizo	138	Kakuzan
036	Bishoku Maimon	142	Gion-ro
040	San Nen Buta-Zo	146	Harden Tighten
044	Otooto	150	Kamakura
050	The Stranger	154	Alice's Labyrinth
056	Simpatica	158	Teiryou
060	Le Porc de Versailles	162	Yui
064	Alux	166	Koyoshigure
068	Thai Thai Yamagata	170	Yanbaru
074	Bu'sa	174	Seoul Soul
080	Maimon	180	Ugoku Machi
084	Shirokakuya	186	Restaurants: Addresses
088	Hirari	188	Architects & Designers: Index
092	Luxis	190	Poems: Translation
098	Gets'ka	192	Acknowledgements

目次 *Contents*

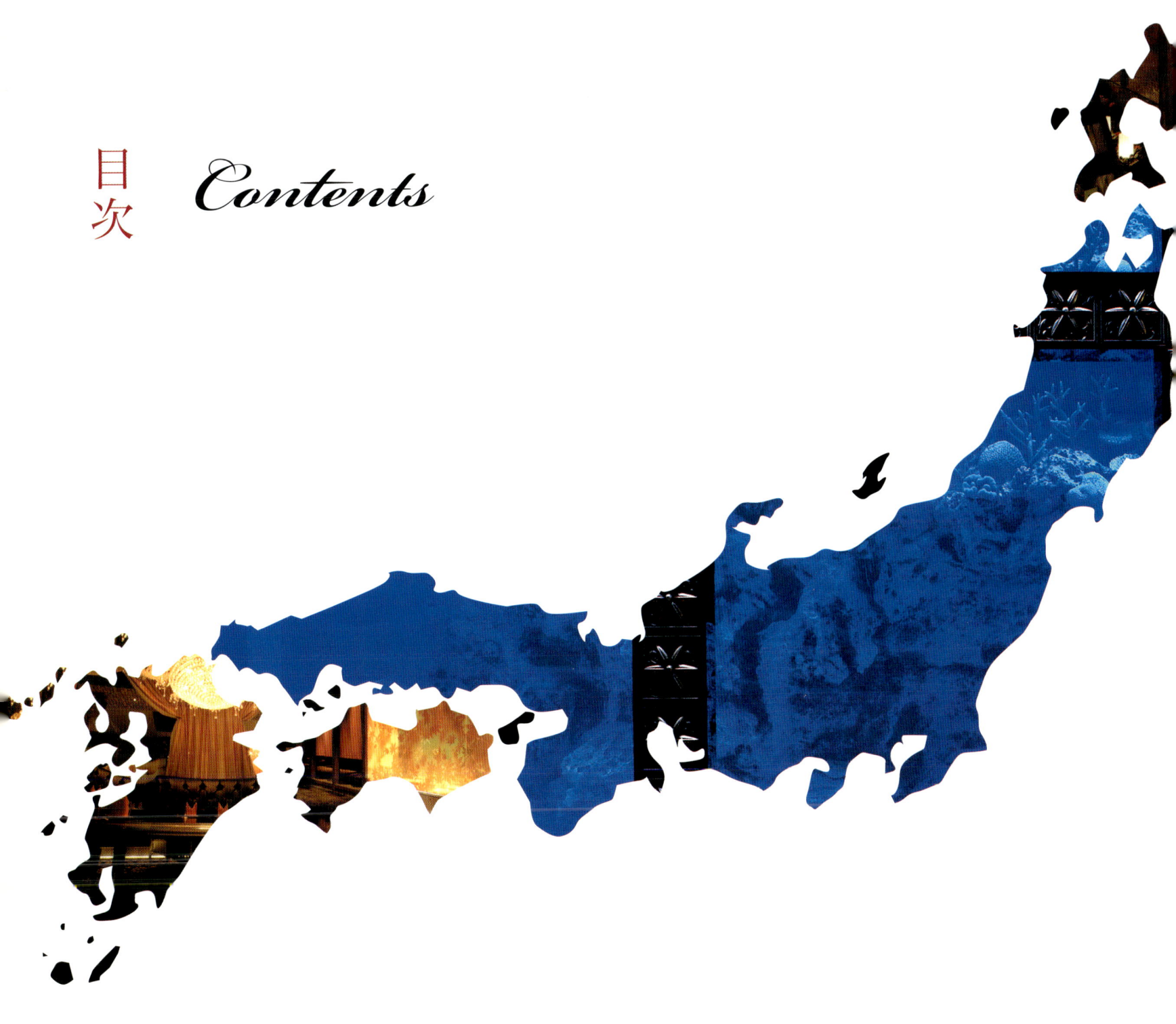

HIP
DINING

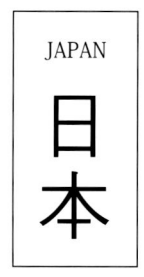

JAPAN

日本

ELLEN NEPILLY

LINKS

Published in 2008 by
Page One Publishing Private Limited
20 Kaki Bukit View
Kaki Bukit Techpark II
Singapore 415956
Tel: (65) 6742-2088
Fax: (65) 6744-2088
enquiries@pageonegroup.com
www.pageonegroup.com

Editorial/Creative Director
Kelley Cheng

Editor
Elaine Lee

Author
Ellen Nepilly

Graphic design & editorial coordination
Adelien Vandeweghe

Japanese Copywriting
Junichi Yanagisawa

Translation of Japanese Copywriting
Ellen Nepilly

Proofreading
Joyce Sim

All rights reserved. No part of this publication may be reproduced, stored in any retrieval system or transmitted, in any form or by any means, electronic, mechanical, photocopying, recording or otherwise, without prior permission in writing from the publisher.
For information, contact Page One Publishing Private Limited, 20 Kaki Bukit View,
Kaki Bukit Techpark II, Singapore 415956.

Printed and bound in China

HIP DINING JAPAN
Copyright © 2008 Page One Publishing Private Limited

First published in 2008 by:
Links International
Jonqueres, 10, 1-5
08003 Barcelona, Spain
Tel: +34 93 301 21 99
Fax: +34 93 301 00 21
E-mail: info@linksbooks.net
www.linksbooks.net

Distributed by:
Links International
Jonqueres, 10, 1-5
08003 Barcelona, Spain
Tel: +34 93 301 21 99
Fax: +34 93 301 00 21

ISBN 978-84-96263-93-2

HIP DINING

JAPAN

日本

LINKS

YOON